HEINEMANN
SCHOOL
MANAGEMENT

Appraisal and your School

IVOR GODDARD
AND CHRIS EMERSON

HEINEMANN
SCHOOL
MANAGEMENT
Appraisal and Your School
Ivor Goddard
Chris Emerson
Heinemann Educational
A division of Heinemann Educational Books Ltd.,
Halley Court, Jordan Hill, Oxford OX2 8EJ

OXFORD   LONDON   EDINBURGH
MADRID   ATHENS   BOLOGNA   PARIS
MELBOURNE   SYDNEY   AUCKLAND   SINGAPORE   TOKYO
IBADAN   NAIROBI   HARARE   GABORONE
PORTSMOUTH NH (USA)

A catalogue record for this book is available from the British Library

ISBN 0 435 80651 3

Printed in Great Britain by Clays Ltd, St. Ives plc.

Contents

SECTION I: THE ISSUES OF APPRAISAL

1 The concept of appraisal

Introduction

What makes a good school?

School managers now have at their disposal a whole host of management tools – mission statements; aims and objectives; school development plans; policies for curriculum, assessment, equal opportunities; marketing plans; quality audit systems. All these help the school to define its purposes and to deliver quality education.

But it is the capability of the teaching force which is most crucial to the delivery of the school's aims, to the calibre of the education offered, and to the quality of the educational outcomes. The main task of teachers is to help children to learn – to assist pupils in acquiring knowledge, skills and competencies. If pupils are successful in achieving these aims, the teachers will also be judged successful and the school will flourish.

The effectiveness of the teaching force is paramount in a school's quest for quality. Appraisal promotes quality by monitoring and improving the effectiveness of each individual teacher and therefore of the staff as a whole.

This book is concerned with the 'whys' and the 'hows' of appraisal – its purposes and focuses. But first, the appraisal of teachers is placed in context. How does teacher appraisal square with what is happening in industry and commerce? How did the proposals for teacher appraisal arise?

Industry and commerce

In teacher appraisal, professionals are observed in the course of their work. This feature distinguishes teacher appraisal from most appraisal schemes used in industry and commerce, which rarely include planned observation of the employees in the performance of their duties. Such performance tends, however, to be open to normal managerial scrutiny during the course of an employee's work. The manager can comment on that performance as occasion arises, rather than waiting for a pre-arranged situation.

In schools, on the other hand, what a teacher does is not exposed to the same day-to-day scrutiny. Classroom doors often remain shut. Even when they are open, the complex nature of classroom processes, and the subtle interaction of teaching and learning, make it difficult for the impromptu visitor to form a rapid, impressionistic judgement. Further, in industry and commerce, professionals can often be judged by outcome. Clearly, outcomes are important in education, and we have perhaps in the past concentrated too little on them. It is, however, difficult to assess the process of teaching through outcome alone. In the extreme it would mean that we looked only at the pupils, never at the teacher. Perhaps for these reasons, professional observation is seen as a critical aspect of teacher appraisal, whereas it tends not to feature in business.

The typical appraisal scheme in industry and commerce might consist of the following:

- target setting, where targets and performance criteria are established for the period ahead;

- a structured interview, in which past performance is reviewed, and targets are set for the forthcoming year;

- an employee development plan, which outlines the development needs of the staff member, and the training to be offered to support this.

A commercial organization will see an appraisal scheme as benefiting both the individual employees and the organization itself. From the individual's point of view, appraisal defines goals and recognizes success. It allows for the interface between the organization and the individual to be made clear, so that the individual feels an essential part of the organization, bound up in its endeavours and crucial to its success. It gives an opportunity for employees to give voice to their own ambitions and for the manager to recognize potential. It also allows employees to express their own frustrations, to explain the barriers which they see standing in the path of their own effectiveness.

From the organization's point of view, appraisal allows for clear targets to be set and reviewed, and it gives a picture of the performance and potential of the workforce. Managers gain an insight into the realities of the employee's job – they acquire a truer picture of the workforce which they are managing. Appraisal motivates the workforce, and this also is of immense benefit to the organization.

In a commercial organisation the basis of the appraisal scheme usually

lies in objectives or targets. The employee is required to achieve specified targets during the appraisal period, usually twelve months. The
manager will want to see standards maintained in most areas of the
work, whilst looking for definite improvements in others. It is with these
improvements that the targets will be concerned. It is important that the
employee should be able to negotiate the targets being set. Some of the
targets should be challenging, but employees should not feel that any
target is outside their scope. This can only lead to feelings of resentment
and frustration. Of course, in defining targets, it may well be that measures of support, including perhaps further training, will be discussed to
assist in the achievement of the objectives.

It is only fair that the criteria against which performance will be
judged should be clearly defined. This allows the employee to know
exactly what has to be done to meet or exceed the target. In turn, these
criteria can form the basis of a rating scale. The manager may well assess
performance on each objective on a scale of 1 – 5. This assessment then
forms the basis of the appraisal interview, at which performance is
reviewed, before targets for the succeeding period are set.

It may be that performance ratings are given only after the interview;
they may be the subject of negotiation and agreement during the interview itself. Some managers prefer to start the interview by asking
employees to assess their own performance. This can allow the employees themselves to identify any shortfalls and place them in context,
rather than having to defend and excuse themselves under criticism
from the manager.

The final point which should be noted about commercial schemes is
their almost universal link to pay and promotion. This does not necessarily mean that salaries form part of the discussion in appraisal interviews. Indeed, that could well be counterproductive. If salary is a
current and live issue at the time of appraisal, it is usually best to con-
vene a separate meeting.

Nevertheless, the manager will almost certainly take the appraisal
report into account in the next salary review. There may be a direct link
– performance related pay may depend upon achievement of the targets
set during appraisal. The link may be less direct, in that the award of
future bonuses or salary increments will take into account appraisal
findings. (Of course, any increases in pay will depend ultimately upon
the company being in profit.) Similarly, appraisal interviews will alert
managers to the potential of their employees, so that when vacancies
occur elsewhere in the organization, their suitability for the new opportunity will be known.

■ The appraisal of teachers

Appraisal for teachers came on to the agenda as part of the 'account-ability in education' movement. The start of that movement dates back to the Ruskin College Speech of Prime Minister James Callaghan in October 1976.

This speech signalled the end of the hands off approach which Secretaries of State and the Department of Education and Science had adopted towards school management and the curriculum. Previously, the role of central government had been to resource the service and to determine its general shape. Even the policy of the Labour Governments of 1964 and 1966 to move to comprehensive secondary schools was pursued through persuasion and coercion, rather than through legislation. Most comprehensive schemes were approved by Secretary of State Margaret Thatcher in the period 1970–4, when there was no overt pressure on local education authorities to continue the comprehensive movement.

After 1977, influence started to be exerted from the centre, but gently at first. DES and HMI reports, for instance, started to emerge on curriculum matters. They included: *A Framework for the School Curriculum* (1979); and *The School Curriculum* (1983).

The subject of appraisal was first raised in the Green Paper: *Education in Schools: A Consultative Document* issued by Secretary of State Shirley Williams in 1977.

By the early 1980s, many schools and LEAs were experimenting with their own schemes, coming to appraisal through moves towards self-evaluation in schools. This was acknowledged by the 1983 White Paper: *Teaching Quality*; but it also identified the need to go further:

> ▶ '... employers can manage their teacher force effectively only if they have accurate knowledge of each teacher's performance. The Government believe that for this purpose formal assessment of teacher performance is necessary and should be based on classroom visiting by the teacher's head or head of department, and an appraisal of both pupils' work and of the teacher's contribution to the life of the school.'
>
> **(Paragraph 92)**

The move was continued in the 1985 White Paper: *Better Schools:*

> ▶ '... regular and formal appraisal of the performance of all teachers is necessary if LEAs are to have reliable, comprehensive and up-to-date information necessary for the systematic and effective provision of professional support and develop-

ment and the development of staff to best advantage ... with the most promising and effective being identified for timely promotion; with those encountering professional difficulties being promptly identified for appropriate counselling, guidance and support; and where such assistance does not restore performance to a satisfactory level, with the teacher concerned being considered for early retirement or dismissal.

This document formalized the position of the Secretary of State, Sir Keith Joseph. He had expressed concern on many occasions that incompetent teachers should be weeded out. Teachers and LEAs were puzzled by this emphasis. There were already procedures, both formal and informal, by which the poor teacher could be eased out. Teachers' associations suspected a ploy to reduce the number of teachers in line with the decrease in pupils (falling rolls) then hitting schools. As far as teachers were concerned, the positive benefits of appraisal for the purposes of professional development were far outweighed by the prospect of appraisal being used for purposes of advancement, discipline and dismissal.

Discussions between the Government and teachers' associations took place against a background of industrial action in schools to support the teachers' pay claim. The help of the Advisory Conciliation and Arbitration Service (ACAS) was sought in solving the teachers' dispute. As part of its procedures, an Appraisal/Training Working Group was established. The Working Party had available to it a seminal report *Those having Torches* ... from a DES-funded research study undertaken in Suffolk.

The Appraisal/Training Working Party contained representatives of the teachers' associations, the local authority associations and the DES; in June 1986 it produced a unanimous report. The Working Party had certainly veered to the staff development model:

▶ "... what the Working Group has in mind is a positive process, intended to raise the quality of education in schools by providing teachers with better job satisfaction, more appropriate in-service training and better planned career development based upon more informed decisions.'

As far as disciplinary procedures were concerned, these 'would remain quite separate'.

Based on the Working Party's Report, the Government funded an Education Support Grant Project: 'The School Teacher Appraisal Pilot Study'. This project was established under the auspices of a National Steering Group. Pilot work began in January 1987 and was carried out in six local education authorities – Croydon, Cumbria, Newcastle, Salford,

Somerset and Suffolk.

Meanwhile the Government was moving to make teacher appraisal mandatory. The Government ended the teachers' dispute by removing teachers' bargaining rights on salaries and imposing a new contract and conditions of service. These placed on teachers the obligation to participate in appraisal. The Government took power to regulate the appraisal scheme through the 1986 Education (No 2) Act.

The National Steering Group published its report in 1989. Its recommendations were based firmly on the principles adumbrated by the ACAS Working Party. However, the pilot studies provided hard evidence about appraisal which allowed the NSG to build on these principles and produce detailed and refined proposals. In addition, the NSG looked at the resource implications, and concluded that, in addition to initial preparation and training, the cost of operating appraisal in the ongoing phase would be between £36.4m and £40.5m per annum.

The NSG Report was put out to consultation, and in general its proposals were welcomed. By this time, however, the Secretary of State was John MacGregor. He was somewhat less enthusiastic about the concept of appraisal than his predecessors. He announced in September 1990 that although he would establish a national framework for appraisal, participation would be voluntary. He felt that teachers were already under considerable pressure and should not be forced to participate in yet another initiative at this time. (The more cynical suspected that, as an ex-Treasury Minister, he had balked at the cost!)

There was a sense of disappointment in the education world at this decision. The positive nature of the appraisal scheme proposed by the National Steering Group had been recognized, and the potential benefits were seen as providing badly-needed support for teachers at a time of rapid change.

In Autumn 1990 a new Secretary of State, Kenneth Clarke, arrived at the DES. With the change of personnel came a change of policy. Kenneth Clarke announced in December 1990 that he intended to press ahead with appraisal. However, he believed that the NSG had over-estimated the costs involved. Appraisal could be seen as a normal management duty, and the time required for the new scheme could not therefore be viewed as wholly 'new time'. He made available less than a third of the monies recommended by the NSG.

In due course, *The Education (School Teacher Appraisal) Regulations 1991* were approved by Parliament and came into force in August 1991. Appraisal for each teacher would take place on a two year cycle. For at least half the teachers, the first appraisal cycle should start in September 1992. Appraisal for all teachers should have started no later than September 1994.

At the time of publication of the Regulations, there were some claims from the teachers' associations that the Government had reneged on the ACAS agreement and the NSG recommendations. The confidentiality of the teachers' appraisal report was claimed to be compromised, and the distinction between appraisal and disciplinary procedures was no longer clear cut.

Chapter 2 explores how far these claims are true and to what extent the Government's scheme had become one for accountability rather than for support.

2 Why appraisal?

Two models of appraisal

Is appraisal a carrot or a stick? The metaphor is perhaps unfortunate. It creates the picture of the teacher as donkey, reluctantly pulling the cart of education with its baggage of children, weighed down by the national curriculum, local management, and other government-imposed initiatives. In this view, only the promise of future reward, or the threat of disciplinary action, keeps the teacher up to the mark.

It is a picture which most teachers would reject. They see themselves motivated principally by their own high standards and their commitment to the children and students they teach. They deplore the lack of respect shown to their expertise by politicians and the media, they resent the lack of consultation prior to the imposition of yet more initiatives, and they reject utterly the idea that they are driven only by the base motives of greed and fear.

These dichotomous views of the teaching profession lead to two different theoretical models of appraisal – the staff development model and the accountability model. The first model supports teachers in doing their job as well as possible; the second model checks that teachers are doing their job properly.

It may be thought that these two models are at either extreme of the spectrum and that, working inwards, it is possible to produce a blend of the two which contains the best features of both, or at least presents a compromise which is acceptable to all parties. But there are hidden dangers in this approach. The two models are almost certain to elicit diametrically opposed attitudes from teachers. If the two models are amalgamated, teachers will view the hybrid scheme with confusion and suspicion.

The appraisal scheme laid down by statute appears to be built on staff development foundations but to incorporate accountability features. We therefore need to analyse the two models carefully, explore the advantages and disadvantages of each, and then discuss the effect of combining features from the two.

■ The staff development model

The ACAS Appraisal and Training Working Group saw appraisal as

▶ **'a continuous and systematic process intended to help individual teachers with their professional development and career planning, and to help ensure that the in-service training and deployment of teachers matches the complementary needs of individual teachers and the schools.'**

Those Having Torches states that:

▶ **'The cornerstone of appraisal schemes is the belief that teachers wish to improve their performance in order to enhance the education of pupils.'**

In these two quotations we get near to the definition of a staff development model of appraisal. An appraisal scheme starts from the assumption that teachers can improve their performance. This however is not seen as a criticism of teachers. Trainee teachers receive between one and four years of initial teacher education at the beginning of their career. In no way will that training be adequate for a lifetime in teaching. In all professions, in all walks of life, there needs to be a constant upgrading and updating of knowledge and skills. Appraisal forms a structure through which training needs can be identified and satisfied.

**FEATURES OF A STAFF DEVELOPMENT
MODEL OF APPRAISAL**

1 It celebrates what the teacher is doing well.

2 It identifies areas where the teacher may be able to improve.

3 It assists the career development of the teacher.

4 It integrates the school and the individual teacher and identifies areas of mutual interest.

5 It identifies the support and in-service training which the teacher requires in order to progress.

6 It provides the basis for school audit and review.

The first three of these features we shall consider now. The others will be considered in the context of appraisal and the whole school in Chapter 3.

▉ 1 Celebrating what the teacher does well

For most people, job satisfaction and motivation come from the notion of a job well done. Encouragement comes from positive feedback, reward comes from seeing the task fulfilled.

A few people can provide their own feedback. They set their own targets and judge for themselves the outcomes, without needing the approbation of the outside world. Most of us are not that self-sufficient, however. We may not doubt our own judgement, but we need it confirmed. And we need our effort recognized. Virtually everyone thrives on praise. Without that, the well of inspiration can run dry. The spur to our next task is not there.

So where do teachers obtain their feedback? There is one obvious source – the pupils or students. The dawning of understanding on a child's face, a buzz of interest in the classroom, a well-constructed model, a well-argued piece of work, the recognition by a student of his or her personal development, all such signs give constant reinforcement to the teacher. This is enhanced by the interest of parents and the thanks of the students themselves.

Nevertheless, the teacher's life is one of great professional isolation. Whilst there are constant signs of the children's learning, the final outcomes only emerge over the child's lifetime. The effect of one teacher amongst the many who will influence the child; the effect of school amidst the effects of home, friends, media; these are difficult to tease out and isolate. Teachers can never be sure about the lasting outcomes of their work.

Further, most teachers spend most of their working day isolated from other professionals (except where team teaching is the mode of operation). However much discussion there may be in the staff room, in meetings, on courses, this is largely theoretical. Most teachers operate professionally behind closed doors, metaphorically if not physically. They may be visited from time to time by fellow teachers, the head, advisors, but often such situations are artificial, with both teachers and children aware of the unnaturalness of the occasion.

Yet surely it is the judgement of fellow professionals that teachers most respect? They know that teachers who have themselves worked in the classroom can best assess their performance. Praise from someone who *really understands* is the sort of praise which is appreciated. Yet as we have seen, this, ironically, is the one form of feedback that is consistently denied teachers. Pupils' work, comments, reactions there may be. Parents may praise or blame. Even test scores may be used to reflect on teachers' effectiveness. Fellow teachers are largely silent.

So the most valued source of authoritative and meaningful comments on a teacher's work is unavailable. Teachers need to feel that their work is celebrated by the people whom they respect – their peers. Systems to provide this do not exist. Appraisal can supply them.

▌ 2 Identifying areas where the teacher may be able to improve

Appraisal is not a substitute for effective management. Nor is it a surrogate for disciplinary action (on the rare occasions this is needed). As soon as managers perceive a cause for concern, they should take action. The concern may arise from their own observations, or from comments or complaints from other staff, pupils or parents. Whatever the source, the manager should move to investigate and solve the problem as quickly as possible. It is not permissible to defer or refer the problem to appraisal. This would be a dereliction of duty by the manager, and a misuse of the appraisal system.

This is not to say that appraisal may not have a part to play in the process. In investigating a problem, a manager may well feel that the appraisal system can focus on the aspect of the teacher's work which is causing concern. For instance, a teacher's classroom control and discipline might be weak. The manager would no doubt provide immediate assistance, but could also suggest that this be one of the areas to focus on in appraisal. The teacher's difficulties in these areas could then be analysed in some depth and could be the subject of positive help and guidance.

In the main, however, appraisal is more concerned with areas of performance which are not a cause of immediate concern or action, but where, nevertheless, improvement is possible.

These areas may be identified in different ways or arise through different causes:

(i) The teacher is not aware of shortcomings in a particular area. The weakness will come to light during the gathering of evidence, whether that is inside or outside the classroom.

(ii) The teacher is aware of a weakness in performance, but does not know how to remedy it. He or she may therefore ask for this particular area to be a focus of appraisal, in order to be able to discuss the difficulty more fully and obtain help and guidance.

(iii) The teacher is aware of a problem, but believes that its resolution lies outside his or her control. It is perceived as being caused by external factors such as lack of resources or managerial deficiencies. Appraisal can provide the arena for a proper analysis of the problem, and for a reference on to senior management if the source of the problem does indeed lie outside the teacher's own discretion.

(iv) The shortcoming may be caused by the personal difficulties of the teacher – stress or overwork at school, or personal problems which are impinging on work.

Whatever the cause of the weakness in performance, appraisal provides an opportunity to examine the problem dispassionately, to identify causes and to seek solutions.

3 Assisting the career development of the teacher

Appraisal provides the opportunity for self-analysis by the teachers being appraised. It gives them the opportunity to identify their own strengths and weaknesses and to test these against the opinions of an independent observer. A critical friend is often able to act as a mirror, reflecting back qualities and aptitudes of which the teacher is only dimly aware.

Many teachers are, of course, happy with their current role in the classroom. They believe that promotion within a school may mean promotion out of the classroom, where they perceive their main vocation to lie. They may therefore be antagonistic to any element in appraisal which focuses on career development. They may see this as an attempt to put them on a treadmill, onwards and upwards, which they have explicitly rejected.

Career development should not be viewed with such a narrow focus. There are many different openings in schools, some of which are still very much classroom or pupil based – a subject coordinator in a primary school, a personal tutor, a mentor to a student teacher. New challenges offer a fresh stimulus to teachers, preventing staleness, and giving them a wider experience which enables them to see their main work in a different light.

Appraisal is thus an occasion when the interests of the teacher can be explored, and these can be matched against opportunities and challenges which may be arising elsewhere in the school. For those who wish it, it also gives a chance to look at how the teacher's career is developing, and to discuss what might be appropriate goals in terms of moves and promotions.

■ The accountability model

In its purest form, an accountability model of appraisal would be interested in matters such as those below.

FEATURES OF AN ACCOUNTABILITY MODEL OF APPRAISAL

1 It identifies incompetent teachers.

2 It identifies weaknesses in a teacher's performance.

3 It assesses performance for purposes of pay and promotion.

4 It provides evidence for any disciplinary procedures.

■ 1 Identifying incompetent teachers

It was Sir Keith Joseph who first put appraisal high on the Government's agenda. He was driven, apparently, by a desire to eradicate what he perceived as large numbers of incompetent teachers who were causing our schools to fail.

Today, the task of identifying and dealing with any teacher incompetence lies firmly with the school. Local management of schools has put the power of hiring and firing into the hands of the governors and the headteachers. It would only be at their behest, therefore, that an appraisal system would be used to identify incompetence.

We have already noted that appraisal is not a substitute for effective management, and that unsatisfactory performance by teachers should be dealt with through normal management procedures rather than awaiting appraisal. A senior management team that depends upon appraisal to identify incompetence may itself be incompetent. Appraisal to identify incompetence may therefore be of little significance. Nevertheless, teachers' perceptions are important. If they see appraisal as having this somewhat negative purpose, their own reactions to the scheme may well be negative.

■ 2 Identifying weaknesses in a teacher's performance

Identifying weaknesses is a matter of emphasis and purpose. 'Identifying areas where the teacher may be able to improve' was one of the features of a staff development model of appraisal. The purpose of this identification was wholly positive – to give support and guidance to the teacher to bring about improvement. Where, on the other hand, the purpose of identifying weaknesses is to help determine pay or to start disciplinary proceedings, it may be difficult to obtain teacher cooperation in the scheme.

3 Assessing performance for purposes of pay and promotion

There are good reasons for organizations to reward those employees who perform well. This motivates everyone to give of their best, and ensures that the most competent remain with the organization. Appraisal which is directed towards identifying good performance, and towards the setting and meeting of targets, seems ideally suited to contribute to performance-related pay. Indeed, many industrial and commercial appraisal schemes link directly with pay and promotion, and staff perceive this as perfectly reasonable and fair.

There are three problems with this system. First, linking appraisal to pay significantly alters the attitude of teachers to the process. They must now present themselves in the best possible light. No longer is it in their interests to expose problems in the hope of receiving help and support. Such difficulties must be swept under the carpet. No longer is appraisal a partnership between the appraiser and teacher discussing professional practice. Instead, teachers need to market themselves, whilst appraisers need to look carefully below the surface of what is being presented.

The second difficulty relates to the criteria to be used to award the performance-related element of pay. If the targets set during appraisal are to be the determinant, then there must be comparability of targets between teachers. In these circumstances, targets are less likely to be addressed to the professional needs of individual teachers and the children in their care. Instead, there is likely to be a concern to set targets of the same 'standard' across the staff. Even here, there is great potential for discord and dispute between staff as to the way in which targets are set, and their accomplishment is judged.

The third difficulty concerns the operation of a performance-related scheme. A good school will have in place salary policies and structures which reward staff fairly and maintain appropriate differentials. The school will thereby hope to recruit, motivate and retain staff of high calibre. For most schools, there is little enough money within the available budget to provide such structures. There is unlikely to be money left over for bonuses. In these circumstances, any element of performance-related pay can only be found by depressing the basic levels of what are considered to be the appropriate staff salaries. In other words, teachers would have to perform to the maximum of their potential in order to earn their normal salary. This is hardly how performance-related pay works in industry and commerce, where the extra payment is generally regarded as a bonus for additional targets reached.

It is difficult for schools to increase their productivity. A widget manufacturer might raise efficiency by installing new machinery. The same workforce might then produce 20% more widgets in the same time. The additional profit thus generated would pay for their bonus. A school's teaching force cannot increase its throughput of children in the same way, unless it increases the number of children in each class. Where a school is successful and attracts more pupils, the extra income received will have to be spent in employing additional teachers, in order to maintain the teacher – pupil ratio. There may of course be some marginal gains. Some classes, some option groups, particularly in the sixth form, may not be full; extra students will be accommodated without increasing the teaching complement. In general, however, schools will not be able to generate income for performance-related pay through greater efficiency or productivity. The money will have to be carved out of the original budget.

There is an alternative – for schools deemed to be performing well to be rewarded with extra income. This could then be distributed within the school on a performance-related basis. To be accepted as fair, such a system would need to be based on a wide spectrum of performance indicators, judged on a value-added basis.

4 Providing evidence for any disciplinary procedures

From the manager's point of view, it will seem perfectly logical to use any relevant evidence during disciplinary procedures. Appraisal results might seem particularly useful, since the processes will have concentrated in some depth on the teacher's performance. The same difficulty arises, however, as with pay and promotion. If teachers suspect that any evidence arising from appraisal may count against them, their attitude to the appraisal process will be completely different.

Are the two models for appraisal compatible?

The compatibility of the two models – the professional development model and the accountability model – will depend upon the attitudes which teachers are likely to adopt in undergoing appraisal in each of them.

In the professional development model, appraisal is a genuine two-way process between the appraiser and teacher. It takes place in an atmosphere of trust and confidentiality, and self-appraisal is at its heart. If this model is to succeed, it requires that teachers should be: open; honest; self-critical during the process; willing to comment frankly on their perceptions of their own strengths and weaknesses and those of the management; open to constructive criticism and to pointers to self-improvement.

The accountability model fosters defensiveness. It implicitly encourages teachers to defend their own position, to hide any weaknesses, and to blame management or others for any deficiencies in their performance. In setting targets, teachers will be looking to their own interests rather than those of the school or their pupils, and they will try to negotiate targets which are as unchallenging as possible. In commenting on their own performance, teachers will tend to inflate their actual achievements. This model therefore encourages teachers to serve their own interests and to maximize their own position.

Teachers will bring to the two models totally different perceptions and attitudes; it is clear, therefore, that the two are not compatible.

How far does the statutory scheme accord with one model or the other? The aims of appraisal, as laid down in the *Education (School Teacher Appraisal) Regulations*, are listed on pages 35-6 of this book.

The aims are unexceptionable. They reflect the aims listed in the ACAS Report (which was agreed by all parties) and for much of the text the wording is identical. Even the potential need to draw on relevant information from the appraisal records for disciplinary procedures is recognized by the ACAS Report. The main difference is the ability granted to managers to draw on appraisal records 'in advising . . . on the use of any discretion in relation to pay'. In other words, appraisal can be used as part of a performance-related pay system. This point was immediately seized upon by the teachers' associations.

> ▶ 'Now we know. Appraisal can be used to determine the pay of teachers. It is no longer about professional development, strengthening weaknesses and building on strengths. The Government's aim is for it to be used to cut pay. The saving thus made is then to be used as merit pay.'
>
> (Doug McAvoy, NUT General Secretary in the *Times Educational Supplement* 16 August 1991)

This somewhat overstates the case. Professional development is still well to the fore in the statutory scheme. However, the concept of performance-related pay for the teaching profession is being actively explored by the School Teachers' Review Body. The Regulations have therefore at least left the door open to the possibility of a link between appraisal and pay. What may not be realized is how such a link could foul the waters. If performance-related pay becomes a reality, and appraisal is linked to it, teachers may no longer approach appraisal in an open, honest manner. Compared with the imperative of presenting the best possible case in support of next year's salary cheque, professional development will have a much lower priority. Yet if performance-related pay is introduced, there will have to be targets, there will have to be performance indicators, and there will have to be judgements about whether the performance indicators have been satisfied. Is this target setting and assessment to be separate from the appraisal process, with its own goal setting and evaluation? Can we really expect schools, hard pressed for resources, to establish two, parallel, systems? Is it realistic, anyway, to expect headteachers to ignore appraisal reports when they are making judgements? Surely such reports are bound to influence both the thinking and the decisions of headteachers.

Schools are increasingly in the market place. They are more accountable, open to external inspection, and they may be judged by the outside world on performance indicators which will include test results and truancy rates. This external pressure is already affecting the ways in which schools arrange their affairs and tailor their image. If external performance indicators become the norm, they are bound to permeate the thinking within the school for better or worse. If performance-related pay becomes a reality, teachers' own targets will inevitably become linked to these external indicators.

In this atmosphere, headteachers will still try to keep a professional vision before their staff, knowing that if the quality of education is high, the external indicators will come right. But there may be a hard struggle to keep professionalism and collegiality to the fore. Appraisal could be the point at which teachers feel most vulnerable in this brave new world, and it could be at this point that professional development first loses out to accountability. Senior managers may need all their powers of leadership and inspiration to make it otherwise.

3 Appraisal in a whole-school context

The school's culture

Pupils' learning should be at the heart of the purposes of every school. The quality of this learning is undoubtedly affected by the ways in which schools organize themselves and operate. Schools with identical resources and similar pupil intakes can nevertheless vary substantially in the quality of learning offered and in the final achievement of the pupils. These differences can ultimately be traced back to the culture of the school.

Each school has its own unique culture, based on factors such as:

- the traditions and philosophy which underpin the purposes of the school;
- the ways in which this philosophy is converted into practice;
- the structures through which the school operates;
- the values and experiences which each person brings to the school;
- the nature and quality of people's actions;
- the ways in which people interact.

For a school to be effective, there needs to be a school philosophy which is clearly articulated. This philosophy should be based on the shared values of the school community, and it should be compatible with the values of the individual members of that community. If this is the case, both staff and pupils are able to feel ownership. The philosophy must also be converted into practice, of course. There should be no discrepancy between what a school says and what a school does.

Yet this ideal is difficult to deliver in practice. All schools now have explicitly stated aims and objectives, delivered through a school development plan. But staff may feel no ownership of these. The management structure may discourage innovation or challenge to the status quo. The attitudes of staff and pupils may be unenthusiastic. Relationships between members of staff, and between staff and pupils, may be poor. Thus there may well be a mismatch between the climate of the school and the desires of the individual teachers. If individuals feel unable to deploy their skills and abilities, they can feel marginalized and unfulfilled. The result is almost certainly demotivation. Yet the success of a school depends crucially upon its human resources. The successful school is one where individual teachers are motivated; where the disparate talents of the various members of staff are harnessed; and where all efforts are coordinated so that the school's objectives are fulfilled.

Appraisal provides a process which can foster this integration of individual teachers with the school as a whole.

▉ Integrating the school and the individual teacher, and identifying areas of mutual interest

Many pilot appraisal schemes have started with a whole school review or evaluation. The school spends some time in defining and reflecting on its current practice. There can then be discussion as to whether this practice actually mirrors people's wishes or intentions. Such an exercise provides the agreed context within which appraisal can take place. Each teacher has had a part in formulating the overall framework.

Whether or not schools choose to introduce their appraisal scheme through such a whole-school review, there is little doubt that the appraisal procedure itself will reflect on and illuminate processes within the school.

In their report *Developments in the Appraisal of Teachers* (DES, October 1989) HMI noted that:

▶ '... over one-third of the institutions – a growing proportion since autumn 1988 – said that staff appraisal provided an opportunity for institutional development and change. Several saw it as a means of matching institutional and individual interests. Communication, both in terms of what was going on and of feeding back the staff's perceptions to senior management, was also seen as an important aim. The monitoring of progress and curricular and departmental reviews were also mentioned, as were other management processes such as target-setting and the writing of job descriptions ...'

Thus, for individual teachers, appraisal provides an opportunity to reflect on how their own skills and qualities can be moulded and adapted to fit the school's overall agreed purposes. It gives them an opportunity to match their objectives with those of the school, to explore differences, and to seek ways in which the two sets of purposes can be aligned. Similarly, it provides an occasion for teachers to bring out and offer those skills, talents, ambitions, which they feel the school is currently failing to use. Appraisal can therefore provide scope for individual teachers to integrate themselves more closely into the school.

From the school's point of view, appraisal can form a very valuable strand in its own self-evaluation. Appraisal will throw up information and judgements from a large number of staff. Many of these judgements will reflect on the school, its purposes, its structures, its senior management, its allocation of resources. They will show where teachers feel unable to work to their own full potential, to satisfy the demands of their job description, not through their own inadequacies, but through failures in the school's management and support structure.

The appraisal process can provide information which, when properly evaluated, may show:

- ways in which the school's culture might be shaped to mirror more closely the aspirations of the staff;
- where aims and objectives might benefit from revision;
- where management structures might need overhauling;
- how the school development plan might be amended;
- how the staff development policy should be revised;
- how staff might be assisted to do their own jobs better.

Properly used, the information arising from appraisal can provide invaluable feedback, and can assist the school to unite and move forward positively.

These benefits will arise only where the school is managed in an open and participatory way. The school management team must be responsive where appraisal indicates the need for change, whether this is in management style, resources, or approaches to the curriculum or to the care of pupils.

The benefits of appraisal

To summarise, therefore, appraisal is capable of bringing a number of benefits to the school and to individual teachers.

Benefits to the school

Appraisal:

- provides a forum for the expression and exchange of ideas and information;
- coordinates staff and school aims;
- clarifies priorities;
- improves communication;
- creates a more supportive environment;
- enables the staff development policy to be aligned to actual needs;
- provides a basis for moving forward the school development plan;
- provides a means of school self-evaluation.

Benefits to the teacher

Appraisal:

- provides clarification of the job;
- offers improved feedback and recognition;
- enables the identification of professional development needs;
- provides advice on career opportunities;
- offers support in work-related issues;
- allows an opportunity to identify external restraints to personal achievement;
- enables greater motivation and job satisfaction.

4 The qualities of a good appraiser

Selecting the appraiser

The DES Circular *School Teacher Appraisal* lays down responsibility for the selection of appraisers and gives guidance as to whom they should be:

▶ **'It is the head teacher's responsibility to select the appraisers of school teachers in his or her school.'**

[Paragraph 22]

▶ **'Wherever possible the appraiser should already have management responsibility for the school teacher.'**

[Paragraph 21]

These quotations imply that the choice is easy, almost automatic. Yet the headteacher needs to exercise some care. The success of the appraisal process depends very heavily upon the calibre of the appraiser. The role is not easy, and not everyone will be qualified to undertake the task. In this chapter we look at the attributes possessed by the good appraiser.

It is essential above all that appraisers should have **credibility** with the persons whom they are appraising. There are two important elements to credibility: **quality** and **legitimacy**.

Quality

Quality within the appraisal process depends upon the personal skills of the appraiser.

PERSONAL SKILLS REQUIRED IN AN APPRAISER

1 Observing

2 Interviewing

3 Listening

4 Questioning

5 Analysing

6 Counselling

7 Facilitating

1   The appraiser must be a skilled **observer**, since the periods of classroom observation are central to the whole appraisal process. Appraisers should

- have a clear conception of the areas on which they wish to focus;

- perform their role without unduly influencing what is happening in the classroom;

- be sensitive to the atmosphere within the classroom;

- be aware of the very wide range of activities and interactions which occur;

- view objectively what they see and hear;

- understand and be able to interpret their observations.

2   The appraiser must be a skilled **interviewer**. He or she must be able to

- create an agenda which addresses the relevant issues;

- structure the appraisal discussion so that these issues are properly addressed;

- create a purposeful but non-stressful atmosphere.

3   The appraiser must be a careful and sympathetic **listener**, concentrating both on what is said and how it is expressed. The appraiser needs to be alert to subtleties and nuances of speech and body language.

4 In conducting the appraisal discussion, the appraiser must be a skilled **questioner**. The questions should be non-threatening; they should be open in form, rather than closed, so that the answers are not predetermined; and they should be posed in such a way that the answers do not just convey knowledge to the appraiser, but also develop self-perception in the teacher being appraised. It is also important that the appraiser should listen carefully to the answers, so that nuances are picked up, and underlying issues are exposed and explored.

5 Prior to the appraisal discussion, the appraiser must be able to assimilate and **analyse** the information received from the various sources. Accurate conclusions can thus be drawn about the teacher's strengths and weaknesses. These then provide a firm base from which issues can be explored, guidance given and solutions reached.

6 Appraisers must also be skilled **counsellors**. They must assist the teachers being appraised to recognise and confront the issues. Where necessary they must probe, explore and expose inconsistencies. But they must also guide, support and advise, commending and reinforcing good practice, helping the teacher to see where solutions to difficulties or weaknesses may lie and negotiating reasonable targets for the future.

7 Finally, appraisers should act as **facilitators**, helping the teacher access the resources, counselling and staff development which they need.

■ Legitimacy

Legitimacy within the appraisal process depends upon the appraiser having the qualities shown in the table below.

QUALITIES REQUIRED IN AN APPRAISER
1 Competence
2 Knowledge
3 Experience
4 Authority
5 Time

1   The appraiser must be acknowledged as a **competent** practitioner
    in the area which is being appraised. Confidence in the appraisal
    system will be totally undermined if the appraiser's expertise is in
    question.

    For instance, it may be known that an appraiser has poor class-
    room management skills, or uses narrow or outdated teaching
    methods. Teachers are unlikely to take seriously comments made
    by this appraiser about their own methods and practices.

    The headteacher must take this factor into account in allocating
    appraisers. Particular difficulties may arise where the line man-
    agement structure is being used to assign appraisers. The staff
    within a particular subject department, for instance, may have lit-
    tle confidence in the head of department. The prospect of being
    appraised by this head of department may bring disenchantment,
    resentment or even outright rebellion.

2   The appraiser must also possess the requisite **knowledge**. When
    the appraisee is a classroom teacher, the knowledge involved is the
    subject knowledge and teaching methods pertinent to that subject.
    This may cause particular problems for the appraisal of heads of
    department or curriculum coordinators. Can a deputy head in a
    secondary school with, say, a background in humanities appraise
    the classroom teaching of the head of the science faculty? Can a
    head in a primary school judge the quality of advice and support
    being given by the technology coordinator?

    It could be argued that a teacher with wide experience is capa-
    ble of going into any classroom and drawing accurate conclusions
    about the validity of the teaching and learning taking place. Often
    HMI, and LEA inspectorates where the LEA is small, work on the
    principle of doubling up subject responsibilities. Of course, in
    such situations, the inspectors concerned will make considerable
    efforts to come to terms with their 'new' subjects. In schools, it
    may not be reasonable to expect appraisers to make the same exer-
    tions. All senior managers in schools have, to some extent, to be
    polymaths; it is also true that an experienced teacher will be able
    to make valid judgements about most classrooms. Nevertheless,
    where the appraiser is working outside his or her area of subject
    expertise, there is a danger that crass judgements will be made,
    and that weak or inappropriate advice will be given. When this
    happens, the teacher is likely to lose faith in the whole appraisal
    procedure.

3   The necessity for the appraiser to have appropriate **experience** is
    part of the same picture. This point has been well borne in mind

with respect to headteachers. One of the headteacher's appraisers must be someone who is, or has been, a headteacher with experience relevant to the current conditions in the school of the headteacher being appraised.

How does this point affect the classroom teacher? All appraisers will be experienced in the classroom. However, the experience may not be considered directly relevant. For instance, early years teachers may feel uncomfortable with an appraiser who has taught only older children in a primary school. A special needs teacher might consider that an appraiser without experience in this area will be unable to make valid judgements or give worthwhile support. The same dangers are inherent as were discussed in terms of subject knowledge: that inappropriate conclusions will be reached, that constructive guidance will be unavailable. The legitimacy of the whole process will then be called into question.

4   The appraiser will also need the necessary **authority** to carry through any recommendations emanating from the appraisal process. The appraisal outcomes may point to staff development needs, to resource requirements, or to the necessity for managerial changes. Appraisers should be wary of giving any commitments during the appraisal discussion which are not directly within their power to grant. At best, targets which depend upon action or resources from elsewhere should only be agreed conditionally. Having said that, frustrations are likely to arise where appraisal has identified needs which cannot subsequently be met. Ideally, the authority of appraisers should be such that, even if power is not directly in their hands, then at least their influence is likely to bring about the desired outcomes.

5   Finally, the appraiser requires **time**. Recent and ongoing innovations in schools have already overloaded teachers in general, and managers in particular. Appraisal may be seen as yet another task which the managers have to absorb. Indeed, the resource situation in school may make any other solution difficult. In this case, there is a grave danger that an appraiser will have little alternative but to rush the whole process. Yet this could invalidate appraisal in the eyes of the teacher being appraised.

One can envisage events which may occur – inadequate information gathering; hurried preparation for the classroom observations; late arrival in the classroom; postponement of the observation sessions or the appraisal discussion; interruptions during the appraisal discussion itself. All senior managers will recognise the scenario where a crisis elsewhere causes an immediate adjustment of priorities. If this occurs during the appraisal process, however, it is likely to prove fatal to the confidence and commitment of the teacher being appraised.

Appraisal will be both important and stressful to the teacher. If the teaching session for which he or she has so carefully prepared is cancelled; if the appraiser shows lack of concentration; if the discussion is broken into at the point where the teacher is coming to terms with difficulties or inadequacies... all such occurrences will cause teachers to distance themselves from the whole procedure, to put up the shutters. Because the appraisal process touches such sensitive nerves, it is essential that the appraiser finds the necessary time, and allocates total priority to any commitments entered into with the teacher being appraised.

■ Equal opportunities

Women teachers form a majority of the teaching profession. In the infant years, there is an overwhelming predominance of women teachers. The same is only slightly less true overall in the primary sector. Even in secondary schools, women teachers are still in the majority. However, when one looks at the number of senior managers, the position is reversed. The proportion of male teachers in the primary sector who are either heads or deputy heads is over 50%. Only 15% of women are in such senior posts. The same picture is reflected down through the positions of responsibility.

Where appraisal is carried out through the management structure, it is obvious that men will be appraisers more frequently than women, and that for a large proportion of the time, men will be appraising women. What are the issues associated with this fact?

Sexual stereotypes can be misleading. Nevertheless, if we do not take account of the different attitudes and approaches which men and women bring to life and work, appraisal may never create a proper dialogue. There will be no actual meeting of minds. We therefore take a brief look at this issue, recognising that we speak in generalisations, and that these can be misleading in individual cases.

In general, men and women view work differently. Men are much more interested in, and motivated by, financial rewards and career prospects. For many men, the current post is merely the stepping stone to the next. For many women, however, their present post is often an end in itself. Immediate job satisfaction will be important. They will be concerned to create a good working atmosphere and to make a contribution which is valued by those around them. Esteem from their colleagues is important, which in turn boosts their own self-image.

Women often lack self-esteem and confidence compared with men. They tend to overestimate men's qualities and standards and demean their own attributes in comparison. This can lead them to underestimate their own worth and contribution, especially in their attitude to managerial positions. They see their caring qualities as more suited to working directly with children; they perceive men's assertive nature as more appropriate to leadership and management.

Where the appraiser is male and the teacher is female, there are potential difficulties of which both need to be aware. If the teacher is concerned that her perceptions of her own role will be rejected or undervalued by the appraiser, she is unlikely to be open and forthcoming. The appraisal will be carried out in a negative, mistrustful atmosphere. The usefulness of the appraisal may also be reduced by a sense of chivalry in the appraiser, who may consider it unreasonable to offer other than bland, toned down comments. This may be reinforced by a feeling that women cannot take criticism. In terms of career development, the appraiser may reinforce the teacher's image of women as poor managers. There may therefore be no encouragement for the teacher to develop her own management and leadership potential.

Equally, however, there can be problems when the teacher does not conform to stereotype. A male appraiser may well feel threatened by, or resentful of, a female teacher who is confident and challenging. Levels of assertiveness which are perfectly acceptable in a male, can be seen as overly aggressive in a woman teacher. This in turn can make the appraiser more negative and judgemental.

Cases of a female appraiser and a male teacher will be less common, but certainly not rare. The appraiser may initially be diffident about offering comment and criticism because of her own perceptions of male superiority. When such feelings have been overcome, it is again important for the appraiser to be aware of the different attitudes to work and career which will inform the male teacher. The teacher must be judged from his own standpoint, not that of the appraiser.

It is therefore extremely important that training for appraisal should cover the issues of equal opportunities and sexual stereotyping. The different stances of men and women must be appreciated so that appraisal is carried out empathetically. Sexual stereotypes should have no place in appraisal. It should be carried out objectively and on an individual basis. Yet if it does not take into account the starting point of the teachers, which will include attitudes and assumptions grounded in their gender, the whole process may become fraught.

■ Who should appraise?

The headteacher has responsibility for choosing the appraisers and the Circular guides the head towards choosing appraisers who have managerial responsibility. This seems appropriate. In some ways, appraisal merely formalizes many of the good management practices which should already be in place. The skills required of a good manager are akin to those required of a good appraiser. Where a manager is not thought likely to be able to appraise well, perhaps further management training is required.

However, heads do have some freedom in this matter and they may certainly decide that the structure for appointing appraisers is one which should be negotiated within the school. Many teachers would actually prefer their appraisal to be carried out by the headteacher. They perceive the head as already being in a position of authority, possessed of wide experience and with both the right and the responsibility for reviewing their work. The head is also seen as being in the best position to remedy any managerial barriers to effective performance, or to allocate the resources necessary for staff development etc. In turn, many heads, particularly in the primary sector, would prefer to undertake all the appraisal themselves. They see it as advantageous to their managerial role, in knowing the competence and qualities of their staff, in supporting them, and in assisting them to overcome any weaknesses or difficulties.

Heads may acknowledge that it is not possible for them to appraise all staff, but they may still attempt to handle the whole burden in conjunction with the deputy head. The Circular advises, however, that no one appraiser should be responsible for appraising more than about four teachers. This seems sensible in the light of our discussion above about available time. For many managers, appraisal will be in addition to their current duties. To take on an excessive number of appraisees would mean either other duties being neglected, or the appraisal process being rushed.

The problem with using a managerial model in primary schools is that the hierarchical structure tends to be very flat. If the head and deputy cannot appraise all teachers between them, other teachers in positions of responsibility may lack some aspects of credibility. The science curriculum coordinator, for instance, may be seen as expert only in that field. This is a matter which needs to be addressed when schools are establishing an appraisal system. The issue of the credibility of appraisers should be discussed so that teachers are willing to accept their appraisers even when the appraisers' actual managerial responsibility for the appraisees is somewhat limited.

In secondary schools, the problem of there being insufficient managers may arise less frequently (although in larger departments, heads of department will be unable to appraise all their staff).

There is a serious question as to whether the teacher should be allowed any element of choice. We have argued that appraisal needs to be based on confidence and mutual trust. There could be occasions on which the head teacher allocates an appraiser whom the teacher finds anathema. The teacher may have no confidence in the appraiser's knowledge, methods or even integrity. There may be personal animosity between the two. In such situations, appraisal is unlikely to be a positive experience. The process will be carried out in a negative atmosphere, full of resentment and suspicion. There does therefore seem good reason to build into the system a method whereby the teacher can request a change of appraiser. Such a request is unlikely to be made lightly because the mere act of asking for change is likely to cause some embarrassment, if not irritation, to the appraiser. Nevertheless, it does give the teacher the opportunity to turn what would definitely have been a negative experience into one with more potential.

SECTION II: THE GOVERNMENT'S REQUIREMENTS

5 Regulations and Circular

In April 1991, the Department of Education and Science produced drafts of the Regulations which the Secretary of State proposed to make on the appraisal of school teachers, and of the Circular to accompany the Regulations. These were sent for comment to local authorities, teacher unions, governing bodies of grant-maintained schools, representatives of voluntary aided schools, and other relevant bodies.

Following consideration of the comments received, the Education (School Teacher Appraisal) Regulations 1991 were laid before Parliament on 24 July 1991, and copies of the Regulations and the accompanying Circular (No 12/91) were sent out to local education authorities. Sufficient copies were despatched to enable one copy of each to be distributed to every school maintained by the local education authority.

These documents covered a range of issues, including the aims and scope of appraisal, responsibilities for its implementation, and the procedures to be used. While the Regulations and Circular cover both teacher and headteacher appraisal, we will deal only with those aspects which relate to the appraisal of teachers.

■ What are the aims of appraisal?

The aims as set out in the Regulations are to assist:

- school teachers in their professional development and career planning; and

- those responsible for taking decisions about the management of school teachers.

In carrying out their duties to secure the regular appraisal of their teachers, local education authorities (governing bodies in grant-maintained schools) are expected to aim to improve the quality of pupils' education, by assisting teachers to realise their potential and to carry out their duties more effectively.

The more specific aims in the Regulations are to:

- recognise the achievements of teachers and help them to identify ways of improving their skills and performance;

- help teachers, governing bodies and local education authorities to determine whether a change of duties would help teachers' professional development and improve their career prospects;

- identify teachers' potential for career development, with the aim of helping them, where possible, through appropriate in-service training;

- help teachers having difficulties with their performance, through appropriate guidance, counselling and training;

- inform those responsible for providing references for teachers;

- improve the management of schools.

Equal opportunities

The Circular stresses the need for appraisal to be seen to be fair and equitable for all teachers. Appraisers will need to be aware of their legal responsibilities not to discriminate on the grounds of sex, race or marital status when conducting appraisals.

Appraisal should be used to promote equal opportunities by encouraging all teachers to fulfil their potential. This includes the encouragement of women teachers and those from ethnic minorities to consider applying for managerial posts, if they have potential.

How does appraisal link with whole-school development?

The Circular stresses the need to set appraisal within the context of the objectives of the school, and particularly the school development plan. Appraisal should support the school's planning, and vice versa. The school's targets each year should be linked with appraisal, so that targets for professional development arising from teachers' appraisals can be related to the targets and priorities in the school development plan. Appraisal targets, when taken together, should provide an important agenda for whole-school action. Targets set during appraisal should therefore meet school needs, as well as those of individual teachers. Setting appraisal within the framework of whole-school development should also make targets established in appraisal more realistic, and make the best use of the resources available.

■ Whose responsibility is it?

The *appraising body* will be responsible for all the aspects of appraisal set out in the Regulations. The local education authority will be the appraising body for its own schools – county, voluntary controlled, voluntary aided schools and maintained special schools. For grant-maintained schools, the governing body will be the appraising body.

The Circular suggests that all arrangements for appraisal should be drawn up in consultation with teachers. Local education authorities will be expected to give schools as much scope as possible within the Regulations to decide on the detailed arrangements for the introduction of appraisal. It will also be appropriate for each governing body to approve the arrangements for its own school. For voluntary aided schools, the appropriate diocese should be consulted.

■ What is the governing body's role?

The governing body of each maintained school has a duty to ensure that the appraisal arrangements are carried out in its school, as far as is reasonably practicable, and to assist the local authority as appropriate. As far as possible, it should be for the school to make the detailed arrangements for appraisal, with the approval of the governing body.

Governing bodies should make sure that they are fully informed of the progress of appraisal within the school, by means of regular reports from the headteacher. These reports should contain a summary of the teachers' targets for action, and progress in achieving these targets. In some cases, appraisal may lead to proposals for the allocation of resources which require the approval of the governing body. Here, the proposals, and the reasons for them, should be reported in full to the governing body so that it can make an appropriately informed decision.

■ Who will be appraised?

As part of their statutory conditions of service, teachers and head-

teachers are required to participate in the appraisal arrangements outlined in the Regulations.

The Regulations apply to all qualified teachers who are employed in
schools maintained by a local education authority or in grant-maintained schools, except for

- teachers with contracts of less than one year;

- teachers employed for less than the equivalent of two days per
  week;

- probationary teachers;

- articled, licensed or other unqualified teachers;

- advisory or specialist peripatetic teachers.

Nevertheless, those responsible for managing teachers in these exceptional circumstances are invited to consider how far the appraisal
arrangements contained in the regulations can be applied to them.

■ Who will do the appraising?

Wherever possible, the person carrying out the appraisal should have
direct management responsibility for the teacher involved. Appraisers
should not, in most circumstances, be responsible for more than about
four teachers. Given this, it may not always be possible for all teachers in
a school to be appraised by their direct managers. In such circumstances,
the headteacher should appoint someone with the necessary experience
and professional standing to carry out the appraisal.

While it is the headteacher's responsibility to select the appraisers,
reasonable requests for an alternative appraiser should not be refused,
where particular circumstances make that appropriate. It is expected
that such circumstances will be exceptional. If there needs to be a change
of appraiser for any reason, the appraisal cycle will continue.

For deputy headteachers, the appraising body may require that there
should be two appraisers. The headteacher will normally be one of the
appraisers. In the case of voluntary aided schools, the headteacher should
consult the governing body about the selection of the second appraiser.

■ Over what period will teachers be appraised?

Appraisal is to take place over a two year cycle. Once appraisal has
begun for a particular teacher, it will be continuous. If a teacher moves

to another school, then the appraisal cycle will start afresh. If the move is to another post within the same school, then it is up to the school to decide whether to continue with the appraisal cycle, or whether it should start again. This decision is likely to be influenced by the extent to which the new responsibilities differ from the old, the stage in the appraisal cycle which has been reached, and whether it is necessary to change the person carrying out the appraisal.

If a teacher is promoted to a permanent post as headteacher, then the appraisal cycle should start again. If the promotion is on an acting basis, then the appraising body must decide whether or not the current cycle should continue.

■ What is the timetable for introducing appraisal?

The Regulations require the appraising body to meet the following targets:

- at least half the teachers for whom it was responsible on 1 September 1991 must complete the first year of the appraisal cycle by the end of the summer term of 1993;

- all the teachers for whom it was responsible on 1 September 1991 must complete the first year of the cycle by the end of the summer term of 1995;

- all teachers who were not the responsibility of the appraising body on 1 September 1991 should start their first appraisal cycle on or before the start of the 1995/96 academic year.

It is for the appraising body to decide how these targets are to be met. Local education authorities will no doubt wish to avoid major fluctuations in costs by ensuring that the number of teachers appraised is spread out over the four year introduction period. Education Support Grants will be available to cover the costs of training and implementation in the first cycle of appraisal for all teachers. £10m of expenditure is being supported in the 1991/2 financial year, with a further £14m in 1992/3. Similar levels of expenditure are expected for 1993/4 and 1994/5.

If a school becomes grant-maintained during the four year introduction period, all teachers who have begun the appraisal cycle should continue with it without any break. Because the governing body of the grant-maintained school will become the appraising body, teachers who have not started their appraisal cycle when the change of status occurs will not have to begin appraisal until September 1995. Governing bodies will, of course, be free to introduce appraisal for their teachers before this date.

■ What methods will be used?

The appraisal regulations **require** the following components:

- classroom observation;
- an appraisal interview;
- the production of an appraisal statement;
- follow up, including a review meeting.

Three other components are **suggested**, but are not compulsory:

- an initial meeting between the appraiser and teacher;
- self-review by the teacher;
- collection of data from sources other than classroom observation.

■ Initial meeting

The Circular suggests that it may be helpful to begin the appraisal process with a meeting between the teacher and the appraiser. The purpose of this meeting would be to plan and prepare for the appraisal. This would be of particular value where the appraiser is unfamiliar with the teacher's work.

■ Self-appraisal

As part of the preparation for their appraisal, the Circular suggests that teachers should be encouraged to recognise the value of self-appraisal of their work, and to carry it out. Where it does take place, self-appraisal should inform all parts of the appraisal process and, in particular, the appraisal interview.

■ The appraisal interview

The interview should be an opportunity for genuine dialogue

between the teacher and the appraiser. It should involve the following components:

- further consideration, where appropriate, of the teacher's job description;
- review of the teacher's work, including identification of successes and areas for improvement or development since the last appraisal;
- discussion of career development, where appropriate;
- discussion of the teacher's professional development needs;
- discussion of the teacher's role in, and contribution to, school policies and management, and any constraints which the operation of the school places on him or her;
- identification of targets for action and development;
- clarification of what is to be included in the appraisal statement.

Targets should focus on the performance, training and development of the teacher. They should take account of available resources and support, and be realistic, precise and capable of being monitored. It is expected that teacher and appraiser will agree on the targets to be set; where this proves not to be possible, the appraiser is able to set the targets. In such circumstances, the teacher is entitled to record comments on the appraisal statement within 20 working days.

The appraisal interview is likely to be most successful where

- both teacher and appraiser are well prepared and well informed for the interview;
- discussion concentrates on those areas for which information has been gathered;
- the interview is free from disturbance or interruptions.

■ What will be appraised?

Appraisal should be based on an established job description. A major focus will, of course, be on classroom practice. However, the appraiser is entitled to deal with all the professional duties undertaken by the teacher, including temporary responsibilities. The appraisal is likely to be more purposeful if it focuses on specific areas of work. This is particularly the case with headteachers, but also so with deputy headteachers and other teachers with a wide range of managerial duties.

■ Classroom observation

Teachers will normally be expected to be observed while teaching on two or more occasions, and for a total of at least one hour.

It is made clear that the appraiser should be familiar with the context of the lesson before observation takes place. To ensure this, it will be necessary for the teacher to brief the appraiser before the lesson. Equally, appraisers should provide feedback to the teachers about their impressions of the work observed. They should aim to do this within two working days of the lesson observed.

■ Other sources of information

The Circular suggests that, while classroom observation is a particularly important source of information, other sources should be taken into account, including the work and progress of pupils.

The Regulations require that appraisers should consult with the teacher being appraised if it is proposed to talk to other people to obtain information for appraisal. The teacher should have the opportunity to give his or her views about who should be asked to provide information and the methods to be used. The appraiser may wish to seek information from other teachers in the school and, in special cases such as a teacher with particular responsibility for home-school liaison, with parents.

In collecting information for appraisal, appraisers should follow the *Code of Practice* which is given as an appendix to the Circular.

■ Code of Practice

The Code of Practice covers the collection of information from sources other than classroom observation. It contains a number of general principles.

- Information collection should be designed to assist discussion in the appraisal interview.

- If it has been agreed that the appraisal will focus on specific areas of the teacher's work, the collection of information should focus on those areas.

- Appraisers should act with sensitivity, and avoid bias in the collection of information.

- Those providing information should not be put under any pressure, other than to respond with accuracy and relevance.

- General comments should be supported by specific examples.

- Interviews should be held on a one-to-one basis.

- Any information received anonymously should not be used.

- Only information related to the professional performance of the teacher should be sought or accepted.

- Teachers being appraised should not adopt an obstructive attitude to reasonable proposals for collecting information.

- Appraisers and teachers should not act in a way that is likely to threaten the trust and confidence between them.

The Code of Practice also points out the need for appraisers to be familiar with relevant national and local education authority policies and requirements. The appraiser will also need to consider a range of background information, including the teacher's job description and school documentation: for example, the school's aims and objectives, pastoral arrangements, equal opportunities policies, or departmental policies. The precise information which will be relevant will depend on the teacher's wider professional responsibilities.

The Code of Practice provides additional guidance for appraisers.

- The appraiser and teacher should agree at the initial meeting the information which it would be appropriate to collect, the sources of that information, and the methods to be used to collect it.

- The appraiser should make clear to people providing information the purpose of seeking the information and the way in which it will be treated.

- Those providing information should be encouraged to give fair and considered comments, which they are prepared to acknowledge and substantiate.

- Any written evidence should be confidential to the author, the teacher and the appraiser.

- People offering critical comments should be asked to discuss them with the teacher before they are used as information for the appraisal.

- Except where a personal opinion is specifically asked for, care should be taken that information is sought and presented objectively.

■   **Period of collection of information**

The collection of all information for appraisal, including classroom observation, should normally take place within a period of half a term. The information collected, however, may relate to the whole of the period since the last appraisal. It may be collected through normal management processes, as well as through ad hoc collection.

The appraisal interview should take place as soon as possible after the information has been collected. Enough time should be allowed between the observation of classroom practice and the interview to allow adequate reflection on the observation by both appraiser and teacher. When one of the observations of classroom practice takes place a considerable time before the appraisal interview, it will be necessary to make notes of the observation and the discussions which follow it.

■   On what basis will work be judged?

Appraisal should be set within the context of the duties laid down in the School Teachers' Pay and Conditions Document, the teacher's job description and the teacher's own work. It should not be an attempt to define the teacher's performance against set criteria of good practice. However, appraisal should take account of the policies of the school and, in particular, the objectives set down in the school development plan.

For appraisal to be effective, there will need to be a shared understanding of what is expected of teachers. Local education authorities and, in the case of grant-maintained schools, the governing body should set out clearly the criteria in teaching and management against which performance should be measured. In doing so, they should take account of national and local education policies, including the National Curriculum, publications of Her Majesty's Inspectorate and, where relevant, the work of teacher training institutions.

Local education authorities will need to consult dioceses about the criteria to be used at voluntary aided schools. They, in turn, may wish to provide additional guidance on the curriculum and other aspects of aided schools to supplement the guidance provided by the local education authority. Maintained schools should also be given this opportunity. All guidance should be prepared in consultation with teachers.

■ What will be in the appraisal statement and who will see it?

The appraisal statement will have two sections:

- a record of the discussions at the appraisal interview;
- an annex, containing the targets agreed at the interview.

The teacher is entitled to record his or her own comments on the statement, within 20 working days, and the teacher, the appraiser and the head teacher should have copies of the full statement. Any review officer appointed to consider a complaint by the teacher should be provided with copies of the existing statements for that teacher.

On request, the headteacher should supply the chairman of governors (not all governors) with a copy of the annex containing the agreed targets, but *not* of the whole statement. For maintained schools, the Chief Education Officer should also be provided with a copy of the whole statement. The targets which relate to professional development needs should also be sent, where appropriate, to those responsible for planning training at school and local education authority level, and, if relevant, to the appropriate diocese.

The Circular stresses the need for all those with access to appraisal statements to treat them as confidential. The previous paragraph specifies those who are entitled to the whole statement or the annex containing the targets. Beyond these, statements should not be discussed with any other person without the consent of the teacher concerned. In very exceptional circumstances, for example where the statement is necessary for legal proceedings or for a police investigation, this requirement may be waived.

The Regulations allow those with access to appraisal statements to use information they contain in making decisions about pay, promotion or disciplinary matters, or for advising others about such decisions. The Regulations *do not* give members of local education authorities or governors (other than the chairman) access to appraisal statements.

Apart from the appraisal statement, all documentation produced during an appraisal should be destroyed once the statement has been produced. The appraisal statement must be retained by the headteacher for at least three months after the succeeding statement has been produced. This is to allow time for the teacher to register any complaint, and for that complaint to be considered, so that the review officer has access to at least two appraisal statements.

The appraising body will need to consider its policy about how long above this minimum period appraisal statements should be kept on file;

the National Steering Group recommended the equivalent of two complete appraisal cycles, a period of four years.

■ How will the appraisal interview be followed up?

Both the teacher and the appraiser have a role in follow-up. The appraiser should help the teacher to achieve the agreed targets, through advice and support; the school will need to have systems in place to assist appraisers in this role.

A review meeting should take place between the teacher and the appraiser during the second year of the appraisal cycle. It should

- review the progress of the teacher in meeting the targets agreed at the appraisal interview;

- consider whether the targets are still appropriate, or whether they should be amended;

- evaluate the training undertaken and discuss the training yet to be received;

- provide an opportunity for the teacher to raise any issues relating to his or her work;

- consider the teacher's career development needs.

The teacher and appraiser should indicate on the appraisal statement that the review meeting has taken place, and record on it any changes to targets and the reasons for the changes. Appraising bodies may wish to include other forms of follow-up within their appraisal schemes.

■ What if a teacher is unhappy with appraisal?

The Regulations set out minimum requirements for complaints procedures. A teacher is entitled to complain about his or her appraisal statement within 20 working days of first having access to it. In the event of such a complaint, the headteacher must appoint a person with relevant knowledge or experience to act as *review officer*, to carry out a review of the appraisal.

The review officer must take account of any representations made by the teacher. He or she may

- order the appraisal statement to stand;

- amend the statement, with the agreement of the appraiser;
- cancel the statement, and order a new appraisal.

If the review officer decides that a new appraisal is necessary, a new appraiser will be appointed by the headteacher.

Beyond these minimum requirements, complaints procedures are formally a matter for the appraising body. A teacher who makes a complaint should be given the right to a hearing, either accompanied or represented by a friend. If there is nobody within the school sufficiently impartial to act as review officer, the appraising body may need to find a suitable person from outside the school. Appraising bodies are expected to have a statement of procedures for making complaints, and to make this available to teachers on request.

How will appraisal link with disciplinary procedures?

Where a teacher is performing inadequately, normal management and communication processes are likely to bring this to light. Appraisal, therefore, is only one opportunity to discuss such inadequacies. Appraisal should be clearly separate from disciplinary procedures, which should be used where the teacher's continued employment is at issue or where there has been some form of disciplinary offence. In such disciplinary procedures, persons who are entitled to have access to appraisal statements may make use of the information they contain.

Chairmen of governors will need to consider their position carefully in the case of disciplinary procedures, because they may have seen the targets from appraisal for the teacher concerned. If they sit on the committee of the governing body which hears appeals against disciplinary action, they will need to take care that their impartiality is not compromised by having seen, and taken action on, any appraisal statement. In such cases, they should take no part in the appeal stage if they have discussed follow-up action to the statement.

Will appraisal be linked with pay and promotion?

There will be no direct link between appraisal and issues related to promotion or pay. It is permissible, however, for headteachers to take into account information from appraisal in advising the governing body on decisions about promotion or pay. In the case of schools without delegated budgets, the Chief Education Officer will be in the same position when providing such advice.

■ How will appraisal be monitored and evaluated?

The government will be seeking information from local education authorities and governing bodies of grant-maintained schools about progress in introducing appraisal. Appraising bodies are therefore recommended to keep records of the progress made. At both school and local education authority level, there will be a need for regular monitoring and evaluation of the appraisal procedures, to see to what degree they are achieving the aims set out for them.

SECTION III: APPRAISAL
IN ACTION

6 The appraisal cycle: an overview

The government's Regulations require that appraisal should take place over a two year cycle, which can be illustrated as follows:

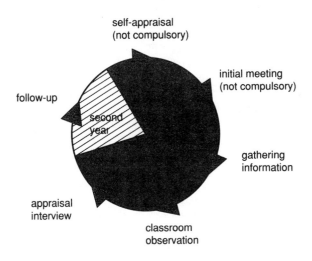

self-appraisal
(not compulsory)

initial meeting
(not compulsory)

follow-up

second
year

gathering
information

appraisal
interview

classroom
observation

The appraisal cycle

The first year of the cycle

In terms of what needs to be achieved during it, the first year of the appraisal cycle is very much the more demanding of the two. It includes gathering of information, classroom observation, and the appraisal discussion, including setting targets and the drawing up of an agreed appraisal statement. We will deal in detail with gathering information in Chapter 9, with classroom observation in Chapter 11, and with the appraisal discussion in Chapter 12. In Chapter 8, we will discuss the areas of teachers' work on which it is appropriate for appraisal to focus.

You will note that two components of the first year of the cycle are not compulsory, self-appraisal and the initial meeting between the appraiser and the teacher. We will discuss these, and why we think that schools should include them in their procedures, in Chapter 10.

The culmination of the first year of the appraisal cycle is the appraisal interview between the teacher and the appraiser. The government Circular makes it clear that the appraisal interview should be 'an opportunity for genuine dialogue'. We do not think that the use of the word *interview* is appropriate for the process of dialogue. Interviews, especially those for teaching posts, are essentially judgemental and competitive. Interviewers see their role as making judgements about the capabilities and personal skills of each interviewee and comparing these for all the candidates in order to arrive at the best person for the job. They are unlikely to know the people they are interviewing, and the purposes of the questions they ask are as likely to be to expose weaknesses as to identify strengths.

The dialogue between teacher and appraiser should be very different; because the appraisal cycle is part of the ongoing management relationship, the appraiser will normally know the teacher well, both personally and in terms of the teacher's day-to-day work. The dialogue should be exploratory and cooperative, rather than judgemental and competitive. It should focus on strengths and future actions, rather than exposing weaknesses. Because of the fundamental differences between the two processes, it is more appropriate to refer to the dialogue between teacher and appraiser as the *appraisal discussion*, and we will use that term for the remainder of this book. We will discuss the skills needed for successful appraisal discussions in Chapter 12.

■ The second year of the cycle

The second year of the appraisal cycle is devoted to following up the targets set in the appraisal discussion and, specifically, to the formal review meeting. When targets are set during the appraisal discussion, and included in the appraisal statement, they imply commitment by both teacher and appraiser to ensure that they are achieved. The Regulations require a formal review meeting, but it is important to understand that the meeting itself will not be sufficient to ensure that targets are achieved. Rather, follow-up needs to be seen as a continuous process to which both appraiser and teacher must contribute. Many of the targets agreed in appraisal discussions will have implications for training and other opportunities for professional development. We will discuss setting targets and how they might be followed up, including meeting professional development needs, in Chapter 13.

■ Related issues

There is anxiety and suspicion amongst some teachers about the use to which the results of appraisal will be put. This is particularly the case where issues of pay, discipline and dismissal are concerned. We will discuss these links, and how anxieties might be removed, in Chapter 15.

Appraisal is a major initiative for schools, at a time when there are many other pressures on time and resources. In order to make the implementation as positive as possible, it is necessary for the school and the staff to be prepared adequately. This preparation calls for a number of management decisions and a range of management tasks. We will discuss these and other issues involved in preparing for appraisal in Chapter 7.

The introduction of appraisal has significant implications for training staff, both teachers and their appraisers. In addition, there are training needs in addressing how appraisal should be managed within the school. Issues concerned with training for appraisal will be considered in Chapter 14.

Finally, as with all initiatives in education, schools will need to give careful thought about how appraisal will be monitored and its effects evaluated. We will discuss monitoring and evaluation of appraisal in Chapter 16.

7 Preparing for appraisal

In this chapter, we will discuss the management tasks which need to be completed to prepare the school and the staff for appraisal. Before doing so, let us spend a few moments considering a mythical school, Ideal Secondary School.

▪ Appraisal at Ideal Secondary School

This school sets great store by its line management relationships. Every member of staff knows who their line manager is and recognises that the line manager is responsible for his or her performance. The parameters of the line management role are clear to teachers and line managers. The teacher knows that the line manager is the person with whom to discuss work priorities, share successes and failures, raise problems and discuss solutions. The line manager provides praise and encouragement, monitors work and progress, gives support and advice, helps in the professional development of the teacher, and agrees to the provision of resources. Interactions between teacher and line manager are frequent, and relationships are built on shared objectives, trust and confidence.

Ideal School has recognised the need for specific job descriptions. Every teacher has one, but the job descriptions are not set in stone; they are updated regularly to take account of the changing responsibilities of the teachers, which themselves reflect changes in the school's priorities.

This school takes staff development very seriously. There are annual staff development discussions for each member of staff with their line manager. At these meetings, teachers have the opportunity to discuss their work, their job descriptions, their professional development needs, and their career aspirations. In order to make the discussions as effective as possible, the school identified the skills needed for teachers and line managers and provided a programme of training for all staff to develop them. Staff development discussions were introduced a number of years ago, and are on a voluntary basis. Initially, only about half the staff opted to have the discussions, but the rest quickly became convinced of their value, and now every member of staff, including non-teaching staff, takes part. They understand the importance of appraisal and, because the staff development discussions have proved to be so helpful in their work and professional development, the prospect of formal appraisal is viewed in a wholly positive light.

The school makes every effort to provide the training and development for teachers identified in the staff development discussions. A range of such opportunities is provided within the school, as well as on courses outside the school. These opportunities include team teaching, job shadowing, taking part in the work of development groups, and acting as a mentor for other staff. Great care is taken to link the development needs of staff with those of the school, and the opportunities provided usually benefit both. The school has tackled the issue of resourcing these development opportunities by including for each target in the school development plan a linked programme of staff development, and the cost of this is included in the resources allocated to achieving the target.

The school bases all its development targets firmly within the context of the learning experiences for its pupils. In doing so, it has recognised the need for a clear understanding of what is required of teachers in the classroom. It set up a small working group to establish criteria for evaluating teaching and learning, involving teachers with a range of teaching expertise and including people at different levels within the school's structure: senior management, heads of department, teachers on the main professional grade, and probationary teachers.

The group started by looking at criteria which already existed, and amended them to suit the school's particular style and needs. After producing draft criteria, there was wide consultation with the whole staff before a final version was agreed. It was recognised that the criteria document itself was insufficient; there needed to be opportunities to put these into practice, so that there was common understanding and interpretation of what was written. To achieve this, a programme of team teaching and observation was undertaken. This involved, in the first instance, pairs of teachers from the same subject department working together in each other's classroom and comparing their perceptions of what took place in each area which the criteria addressed. This was later extended to teachers from different departments, so that a whole school consensus has developed.

Partly through this initiative, but also because of the open and cooperative ethos of the school, visits by teachers to other classes have become a frequent and normal part of school life; this is understood not just by teachers, but also by the pupils. These visits are not seen as threatening; rather, they are perceived as an essential way of sharing expertise and experience, and as good professional development.

The governing body is committed and supportive. Governors recognise the need for, and benefits of, developing the staff. The headteacher has discussed the introduction of appraisal with them and, while they recognise the benefits it will bring to the school, they also understand that appraisal of professional performance must be carried out by the professionals in the school. They see their role as approving the procedures for appraisal to be used in the school, and in allocating sufficient resources for appraisal to be introduced effectively. The governing body, after wide ranging discussions within the school, have clear policies and procedures for staff remuneration, and for discipline and grievance. In meetings with the whole staff, the governors have made clear that there will be no direct link between appraisal and either pay or disciplinary measures.

The school has long been convinced of the need to monitor and evaluate what it does. Evaluation takes many forms within the school, and a variety of people play a part, including governors, parents, pupils and the local community. The results are used to inform the school's planning, particularly in the process leading to the production of the school development plan.

Ideal Secondary School, and one of its feeder schools, Perfect Primary School, which shares many of the features described above, look forward to the introduction of a formal appraisal scheme with relish and enthusiasm. Such a scheme, because it is clearly based on professional development, is merely an extension of what they already do. The headteacher, staff and governors can hardly wait to get started!

If your school is in a similar stage of development – and there are many such – you too will probably be anxious to start appraisal soon. If not, then it is worth considering the preparations that need to be made, and the time it will take to achieve the necessary state of readiness.

One of the factors described above concerns school ethos. This can hardly be described as a management task, but it undoubtedly has an influence on how appraisal is received by staff.

School ethos

Schools vary considerably in their cultures and ways of operating. Some are characterised by openness and consultation, while others reflect a style which is based on hierarchy and direction. Schools use different styles in managing staff. These styles can be described as follows:

- the *tell* style involves instructing, informing, setting deadlines, directing, correcting, setting priorities, and demanding;

- the *sell* style involves encouraging, convincing, getting someone to agree, and persuading;

- the *participate* style involves discussing, negotiating, sharing ideas, cooperating and seeking others' views;

- the *delegate* style involves giving power, authorising, trusting, devolving and encouraging initiative.

It is oversimplistic to characterise schools as using one of these styles exclusively. Schools use different styles in different circumstances, and individual managers use a variety of styles depending on the person they are working with and the issue involved. None of the styles is 'right' and none 'wrong', but it seems likely that a school which operates on the basis of consultation and cooperation will find it easier to introduce appraisal than one in which decisions are handed down from above and where management is predominantly by the 'tell' style. Inevitably, the way that appraisal operates in a school, and how it is received by the staff, will have a close relation to the ethos of the school.

Changing the ethos of a school, even where those with the biggest influence wish it to change, is a long and difficult process; we would not suggest that a school tries to change its ethos simply to make the introduction of appraisal less painful! However, there are a number of things, of a less strategic nature, that schools can do which will improve the climate for appraisal. These are concerned with two specific areas: line management relationships, and classroom observation. Encouraging line managers to use the 'tell' style less, and the 'participate' style more, for example, may lead to teachers feeling less threatened by the appraisal process and, in particular, the appraisal discussion. Equally, encouraging a more open approach to classroom visiting may make the classroom observation component less worrying to teachers.

If we reflect on the factors which make our mythical school ready for appraisal, we can identify a number of management questions which need to be considered. These are concerned with:

- What needs to be done?
- Who will do it?
- When will it be done?

Stage 1: What needs to be done?

The management tasks which need to be undertaken cover the following areas:

1 the school development plan;

2 line management;

3 job descriptions;

4 preparation and training for staff;

5 criteria for teaching and learning;

6 appraisal procedures and documentation;

7 staff development plan;

8 governing body involvement.

1 The school development plan

Embarking on appraisal is a major initiative for any institution, and not least for a school. It requires careful planning and a long lead time. It has implications for training and for resources. It is essential, therefore, that it figures prominently in the school's long-term planning as expressed in the school development plan. Because schools usually aim for no more than five or six areas of development in the plan, and because appraisal is such a major area of development, its inclusion in the plan will, almost certainly, be at the expense of at least one other priority in the school's planning.

Action points:

- review resources required;

- reconsider priorities in development plan;

- decide timetable for implementation;

- consult staff;

- include appraisal in development plan and obtain governing body approval.

---

2 Line management

In order for appraisal to work effectively it is necessary to have a clear line management structure, with one line manager for each member of staff. Line management arrangements need to reflect the management structure of the school; it will often be clear who the line manager of a particular teacher should be. For example, in a secondary school department, it will usually be the teacher's head of department. In other cases, however, it will be less obvious. If appraisal is to be seen as a central part of the line management function, and we believe it must be, in nearly all cases a teacher's appraiser will be his or her line manager. Because successful appraisal is based on successful management relationships, it is clearly important that line management arrangements avoid clashes of personality, wherever possible.

It is necessary here to differentiate between line management and *task management*. A teacher might, for example, have a pastoral responsibility within the school, often as tutor to a group of pupils. In carrying out this pastoral task, the teacher will be responsible to the head of year or head of house. Similarly, some teachers teach in departments other than their main subject. For example, an English teacher may teach in the history department for a number of lessons; in those lessons, the teacher is responsible to the head of the history department for the work he or she does. These responsibilities are specific to the tasks being undertaken, and while they interact with line management responsibilities they do not override them. The line manager retains overall responsibility for all areas of the teacher's work. Making this distinction clear to all teachers should help to avoid misunderstandings.

In addition to clarifying who is to act as line manager for each teacher, it will be helpful to produce guidance, both for teachers and line managers, on exactly what is involved in the line management function. The list of responsibilities might include:

- agreeing and updating the teacher's job description;
- monitoring the teacher's work;
- keeping the teacher informed about developments within the school and outside;
- advising and, in the last resort, deciding on priorities within the teacher's overall job work load;
- praising and encouraging;
- identifying areas for improvement and development, and providing advice and support in achieving them;
- representing the teacher's views in discussions with senior staff;
- acting as a facilitator in the teacher's work, including agreeing to the provision of resources;
- advising on career and personal development;
- appraising the teacher's performance.

Action points:
- clarify line management structure;
- produce guidelines for line managers.

---

3 Job descriptions

The government's circular on appraisal states that 'Appraisal should be undertaken on the basis of an established job description.' The reason for this is quite clear; it is only appropriate to appraise a teacher's performance when what the teacher is intended to do is understood by the teacher and the school.

As a first step, generic job descriptions can be developed, if they do not exist already, for the major job areas in the school. In a secondary school, for example, these might be headteacher, deputy headteacher, head of department, second in department, head of house or year, and main scale teacher. The basis for these generic job descriptions will be the teachers' conditions of service and the school's general expectations of post holders. Once these have been developed, specific job descriptions can be drawn up for each member of staff. This is probably best done through a process of negotiation between teacher and line manager, although the headteacher would no doubt wish to approve the job descriptions once they have been agreed. Job descriptions are discussed in more detail in Chapter 8.

Staff should be clear that job descriptions represent the situation as it is at the time they are produced. They will change with time as the school and/or department's needs change and the teacher develops new skills and aspirations. This concept of *living job descriptions* is a central plank in performance appraisal.

Action points:

- produce generic job descriptions;

- negotiate specific job descriptions.

▉ 4 Preparation and training for staff

While they are not an essential prerequisite of introducing appraisal, many schools have found *professional development discussions* to be a useful way of setting the climate for it. These are voluntary and usually focus on personal and professional development, rather than on performance appraisal; because of this, teachers find them less threatening than appraisal. As well as providing formal opportunities for teachers to explore their professional development with a senior colleague, these discussions can also be of value in encouraging reflection by the teacher on his or her own progress and priorities, and in developing the discussion skills which will be needed for appraisal proper.

In addition to such initiatives which pave the way for appraisal, there is a need for specific appraisal training for all staff. The training needed is of two sorts:

- general awareness training;

- training in appraisal skills.

In any school, the staff will need to have information about the government's requirements for appraisal, the guidance provided by the local authority, and how the school intends to take these into account when producing their own scheme. We suggest how this might be approached in Chapter 14.

In addition to general awareness of the issues involved, appraisal requires skills in a number of areas which may be relatively new to many teachers. First, there are the skills associated with self-appraisal; these are considered in Chapter 10. Second, there are the skills involved in the observation of classroom practice; these are discussed in Chapter 11. Finally, there are the skills needed in the appraisal discussion; these are discussed in Chapter 12.

Teachers need training in all these skills, but most of all they need practice. It is essential that training for appraisal skills is largely directed towards developing skills through practice. Ideas for the content of a skills training course for appraisal are contained in Chapter 14. Some of the skills required are needed for both appraisers and teachers, and some predominantly for appraisers. Despite this, we feel strongly that appraisers and teachers should be trained together and that the content of the training should cover the skills needed by both. This serves not only to develop common understanding, but also to underline the openness and shared approach of a good appraisal system.

Action points:

- decide on content and timetable;

- negotiate with local authority, where appropriate.

■ 5 Criteria for teaching and learning

As part of the planning for the classroom observation component of the appraisal cycle, we believe it is important that there is clear and shared understanding about what appraisers will be looking for when they observe teachers in the classroom. In Chapter 11 we recommend that this should be a whole-school issue, rather than a matter for agreement between individual teachers and their appraisers. In Chapter 11 we also give some advice about how criteria might be established and, once they have been produced, how common understanding among the staff might be achieved.

Action points:

- produce criteria;

- consult staff;

- devise training programme to ensure common understanding.

■ 6 Appraisal procedures and documentation

In developing its approach to implementing appraisal, each school will need to consider what procedures and associated documentation will be required. The school's appraisal scheme will need to contain the following:

- the aims of the scheme;
- roles and responsibilities;
- how information will be gathered;
- how the information will be used, and who will have access to it;
- the procedures to be followed;
- the documents to be used;
- the arrangements for complaints.

In drawing up the scheme, a number of more specific issues will need to be addressed:

- whether self-appraisal is to be included and, if so, what form it will take;
- whether an initial meeting between teacher and appraiser will be required;
- the number and length of classroom observations to be undertaken;
- the approach to gathering information from sources other than classroom observations;
- how appraisal will be recorded;
- the length of appraisal discussions;
- how confidentiality will be assured.

Later in this chapter, we will consider how the associated documentation might be produced, and by whom. At this stage, we will simply list the documentation needed:

- the procedures themselves;
- job descriptions;
- self-appraisal forms;
- criteria for classroom observation;

- a recording sheet for classroom observation;
- an appraisal statement format, including an annex for targets.

Action points:

- devise procedures;
- consult staff;
- obtain governing body approval;
- produce documentation.

▓ 7 Staff development plan

Whether or nor appraisal is seen by teachers to be successful will depend largely on the school's abilities to meet the professional development needs identified through the appraisal process. In addressing these needs, a school will need to have a coordinated approach, preferably expressed in a staff development plan. This needs to be an integral part of the school development plan, and to be linked with other targets within it. Each target in the school development plan should indicate the training needs associated with it, and the costs of that training. The targets for professional development identified in appraisal can then be matched to those identified in the development plan. In this way, the activities and training needed for the professional development of staff can also help the school in achieving its targets.

The training and development activities provided will need to match the particular needs of individual teachers and of the school. Some will best be met by attendance at outside training courses, some by distance learning approaches, and some by development activities within the school. Chapter 15 gives some idea of the range of professional development activities which can be provided at the school.

Action points:

- identify training needs associated with targets in school development plan;
- produce staff development plan.

■ 8 Governing body involvement

There is currently considerable, and perhaps understandable, unease among teachers and their professional bodies about the possible misuse of appraisal in relation to decisions about pay, promotion, discipline and dismissal. In order to allay such fears, it is necessary for governing bodies to develop fair and effective policies in these important areas of personnel management. In devising their policies, or revising their existing ones, governing bodies should incorporate a statement about how the results of appraisal will be used. This issue is dealt with more fully in Chapter 16.

Before entering into appraisal, schools will also need to ensure that their governing bodies are briefed fully about the government's requirements and how these are to be implemented. Particularly, governors will need to be clear about their role, which is essentially one of approving the procedures drawn up by the staff. Many governors may feel that their involvement should extend to taking part in the appraisal process itself, and that a lay perspective would add something of value to the process. It will be an important task for the headteacher to explain why appraisal of professional staff must be left to the professionals within the school.

The Regulations give chairmen of governing bodies the discretion to see the appraisal targets for each teacher. They will need to decide whether they wish to take advantage of this discretion. The six teacher unions have advised strongly that they should not do so, believing that it undermines the essential principle of confidentiality. It is advisable that governing bodies at least discuss this issue and, having made a decision, make their policy known to the staff.

Action points:

- brief governing body about appraisal plans;
- produce policy on pay;
- amend disciplinary and grievance procedures.

■ Stage 2: Who will do what?

Before deciding who should do what within the school, we need to be clear about overall responsibilities for the appraisal scheme. The government's Regulations impose responsibilities on all those involved in the appraisal process, local authorities, governing bodies, headteachers and teachers.

The local authority is responsible for providing guidelines for schools to assist them in producing their appraisal schemes, and for the provision of training. It will also receive information about training needs identified in appraisal discussions in each school.

The governing body in each school will

- approve the procedures for appraisal to be used in the school;

- receive reports from the headteacher about the progress in implementing appraisal;

- receive a summary of the targets identified in appraisal discussions;

- consider and approve plans for action which result from appraisal.

The headteacher will

- decide on the timetable for introducing appraisal;

- consult staff about the procedures to be used;

- appoint appraisers;

- arrange for training, often in consultation with the local authority;

- receive copies of appraisal statements.

All staff should expect to be consulted about the appraisal scheme in the school, and the procedures to be used. They will take part in training and be appraised, and some will appraise other teachers. The in-service training coordinator will receive information on training and staff development needs identified in appraisals.

Coordination

Most schools will find it useful to have one member of staff with responsibility for coordinating the school's development of appraisal. In some schools, especially small ones, this may well be the headteacher. In larger secondary schools, it is more likely to be the in-service training coordinator or a deputy headteacher. The responsibilities of the appraisal coordinator might include:

- establishing and chairing the school's appraisal working group;

- overseeing the production of the school's appraisal procedures and associated documentation;

- planning in-service training for staff, and arranging with the local authority for its delivery;

- giving briefings on developments to the governing body;

- planning and carrying out monitoring and evaluation.

In order to encourage the greatest possible involvement of staff, and to share the workload of the appraisal coordinator, schools may find it helpful to set up an appraisal working group. Careful thought should be given to its composition. It may be sensible to ask for volunteers, but while trying to ensure that the group contains teachers with a range of experience and with different levels of responsibility in the school. With the appraisal coordinator, the group's major responsibilities will be to produce drafts of appraisal procedures and documentation for discussion by the whole staff, and to produce the final versions after appropriate consultation has taken place. The documentation which may be required was discussed earlier in this chapter.

Action points

- appoint coordinator;

- set up working group.

▆▆ Who will be the appraisers?

Careful thought will need to be given about pairing teachers with appraisers. There are three factors which schools should consider:

- relationship with line management;

- manageability;

- trust and confidence.

We have stated in earlier chapters our strong belief that appraisal is part of good management, and that it should involve the person directly responsible for the teacher's work. All other things being equal, therefore, we believe that the equation 'appraiser = line manager' should apply automatically and universally.

There are, however, other factors which may make the adoption of this principle in every case problematic. One of these concerns the workload of appraisers. We must recognise that appraisal – if it is properly carried out – makes heavy demands of time on an appraiser. In recognition of this, the government Circular recommends that, in most circumstances, each appraiser should be responsible for the appraisal of no more than about four teachers. We believe that this advice is sound, but that it should be a guide rather than a fixed rule. For example, in a secondary school department of six teachers, including the head of department, it would be more sensible for the head of department to appraise all five colleagues than to have one teacher appraised by someone who is not directly responsible for their work. Where the guideline figure is to be exceeded, the additional work involved should be taken account when considering the overall workload of the appraiser.

The other factor concerns the benefits of introducing appraisal in as unthreatening a way as possible. Some teachers will no doubt feel apprehensive, despite the efforts that schools might make to allay their fears. If appraisal is to get off to a good start, teachers need to trust their appraisers and have confidence in them. Where this is not the case, the teacher may ask for an alternative appraiser; the government Circular states that 'headteachers should not refuse requests from staff for an alternative appraiser if there are particular circumstances which suggest that this might be appropriate. Such circumstances are likely to be exceptional.' In order to ensure that appraisal starts on a positive note, the headteacher may agree to such a request, but there is a more fundamental problem to be solved – the professional relationship between the particular teacher and his or her line manager.

The six teacher organisations have suggested that, while the headteacher is responsible for selecting appraisers, the 'element of choice is a vital ingredient of any good appraisal scheme'. We do not agree with this view; it seems to us that the general rule that the line manager should be the appraiser should be overridden only where other considerations demand it.

Action point

- appoint appraisers.

Stage 3: When will it be done?

There are three issues to be considered when making decisions about when to introduce appraisal in a school:

1 The government's requirements;

2 Manageability;

3 Readiness.

1 The government's requirements

The Regulations require each appraising body to ensure that the first year of the appraisal cycle is completed for half its teachers by the end of the 1993 summer term, and by the end of the 1995 summer term for the other half.

Remember, though, that this is a requirement for appraising bodies and not for individual schools (except for grant–maintained schools). It will be for local authorities to agree with each school when it will carry out appraisal. Subject to the requirement for half of their teachers to have begun appraisal by the start of the 1992/3 academic year, local authorities will presumably allow each school to decide on the timing which is best suited to its needs. At least in theory, then, a school need not begin appraising its teachers until September 1994. As we will see, however, the decision will also be influenced by consideration of readiness and manageability.

2 Manageability

The second issue which will influence schools' decisions about when appraisal is to be introduced is concerned with manageability. Appraisal, if it is to be carried out in a worthwhile way, will make heavy demands on time, particularly for appraisers. The demands are not evenly spread within the two year cycle. In the first year of the cycle for each teacher being appraised the appraiser will need to make time for

- an initial meeting with the teacher (if it is part of the school's procedures);

- classroom observation on at least two occasions, each involving a meeting before the observation, one after the observation, and the preparation of notes;

- collection of other information;
- preparation for the appraisal discussion, including reading and reflection;
- the appraisal discussion itself;
- the preparation of the appraisal statement.

In the second year of the cycle, the appraiser's load will be in relation to follow-up, including the review meeting. The first year is clearly much more demanding on time than is the second.

Equally, the demands on school resources will be heavier in the first year of the cycle. Time within the school day will need to be provided for appraisers to observe lessons, and for both teachers and appraisers for initial meetings, for discussions before and after classroom observations, and for appraisal discussions.

In most primary schools and in smaller secondary schools it may be feasible to appraise all teachers in the same year. In large secondary schools it would be very difficult to do so. Such schools will probably aim to introduce half of the teachers in one year, and the other half in the following year. For example, a school might choose to begin the first year of the appraisal cycle for half its teachers in the 1992/3 financial year. In the following year, these teachers would complete their first appraisal cycle, while the other half would start the first year of their cycle. In the year after that, these teachers would complete their first appraisal cycle, and the others would begin their second appraisal cycle.

This approach has a number of advantages. Firstly, the school can phase in training for its staff, with each teacher undergoing training in the year before he or she starts the first appraisal cycle. A second advantage is for the school's resources; in each academic year, half the staff will be in the first year of the appraisal cycle and the other half in the second year, so that the demands on resources will be the same from year to year. Finally, the demands on appraisers can be spread out, with each appraising half the teachers for whom he or she is responsible each year.

3 Readiness

The final factor to be considered is the degree to which the school has prepared itself for appraisal. This will depend on how many of the tasks outlined earlier in this chapter have been completed.

We give below a possible timetable for introducing appraisal in a school which is very much starting from scratch. Management tasks are outlined for each financial year; this is in recognition of the need to relate planning to the school's budget. Clearly, schools which have already completed some or all of the management tasks will be able to shorten the lead in period, and make an earlier start to the introduction of appraisal. However, if in doubt, it is probably better to overestimate the preparation time needed than to underestimate it.

▮ A possible timetable

April 1992 to March 1993

- Appraisal included as a major area within the school development plan, with targets for the next four years.
- Line management structure established or confirmed, so that each teacher knows the one person to whom they are directly responsible.
- Guidelines on the role of the line manager produced.
- Briefing to governing body on the government's requirements and the school's proposed response.
- Awareness training provided for all staff.
- Appraisal coordinator appointed.
- Appraisal working group set up.

April 1993 to March 1994

- Criteria for classroom practice developed, after consultation with all staff.
- Staff development discussions introduced on a voluntary basis.
- Appraisers identified.
- Training in appraisal skills provided for all appraisers and for some appraisees – in total, half the teachers trained.
- Governing body produce policies on pay and discipline.
- Appraisal procedures produced, after consultation with all staff.

April 1994 to March 1995

- Appraisal skills training evaluated, and amendments made.
- Other half of staff trained in appraisal skills.
- Half the staff complete first year of appraisal cycle.

April 1995 to March 1996

- Half the staff complete second year of appraisal
- Other half complete first year of appraisal cycle.
- Evaluation of appraisal procedures.

You will notice the heavy demands on time in the earlier years. It may well be that, given all the other pressing priorities that the school must address, such a programme is unrealistic. A more pragmatic approach is needed in such circumstances. It is not essential for all the elements to be in place before appraisal gets under way, although we would recommend that they should be given attention at some stage. It is quite possible to begin appraisal, for example, without specific job descriptions. After all, teachers know the main areas of their job and there are responsibilities laid down in the teachers' pay and conditions document. Similarly, specifically defined criteria for classroom observation are not an absolute prerequisite; within each department in a secondary school, for example, there will no doubt be a tacit understanding of what is expected to happen in the classroom. Again, criteria need not be in a final state, so long as the basic principles are clear and understood by all.

There is, however, a bottom line to what needs to be in place before appraisal begins; openness about the school's approach to appraisal, and trust and confidence between teachers and their appraisers. In any school, if these are not in place then there is a real risk that appraisal will get off to a bad start, and regaining lost ground may prove very difficult indeed. This risk is significantly increased where schools, for whatever reason, have been unable to achieve the management tasks described earlier in this chapter.

8 The scope of appraisal and the job description

Pupils' learning is the most crucial component in a school's activities. This learning takes place largely in the classroom, and the main focus of most teachers' work is classroom teaching. Obviously, therefore, classroom practice must form one of the main areas for appraisal. The role of management is also very important in establishing the framework and environment within which the pupils' education takes place. Appraisal of management duties is not a statutory requirement. Nevertheless, schools would be well advised to include such duties in the appraisal of their senior and middle managers.

There are many aspects to the role of the classroom teacher. Some of these are related specifically to the classroom environment, others to wider aspects of the work.

The classroom role

The following are facets of a teacher's work in facilitating the learning of pupils:

- planning the course;
- organizing the classroom;
- preparing learning materials and activities;
- planning individual lessons;
- undertaking the lesson;
- catering for the individual learning needs of pupils, including those with special educational needs;
- maintaining the learning environment and keeping order and discipline;
- relating to and communicating with children;

- assessing learning outcomes;
- retaining evidence;
- keeping records;
- writing reports;
- liaising with parents.

Wider aspects of the classroom role

In addition to the above activities which are specifically related to work in the classroom, there are a number of other activities which the teacher necessarily undertakes in support of classroom teaching:

- keeping up to date with developments in the teacher's own specialist field;
- keeping abreast of wider educational issues such as assessment, equal opportunities, local management of schools, appraisal;
- communicating and cooperating with colleagues on wider school issues or with respect to individual pupils;
- involvement with extra-curricular activities;
- maintaining attendance and punctuality.

Management roles

A significant proportion of teachers within a school will have specific management responsibilities. The people concerned will include:

- the headteacher;
- deputy heads;
- curriculum coordinators;
- heads of year;
- heads of department;
- personal tutors;
- the assessment coordinator.

Many of these people will carry a substantial teaching load in addition to their management duties. (Some would no doubt prefer to say that they carry management responsibilities in addition to their classroom teaching.) The management role will impose duties and may require qualities additional to those called for from the classroom teacher, including:

- leadership and innovation;
- the management of staff;
- the management of resources;
- management of the curriculum;
- pastoral work;
- appraisal (as an appraiser);
- INSET/ professional development;
- liaison with the community, industry and commerce;
- marketing.

■ What should be appraised?

For the teacher with responsibilities both within and outside the classroom, the range of duties open to appraisal is enormous. An appraisal exercise which attempts to cover all aspects is unlikely to be successful. The data gathering exercise will be vast, the time spent on each aspect will be minimal, the process will be superficial and the outcomes are unlikely to be of value either to the school or to the teacher being appraised.

The DES Circular *School Teacher Appraisal* is certainly clear on this issue:

▶ 'Appraisal is likely to be more purposeful if it focuses on specific areas of a school teacher's work. This will be particularly so with the appraisal of head teachers, deputy heads and other teachers with a wide range of managerial duties.'

[Paragraph 20]

Which, therefore, are the aspects of a teacher's work to be chosen for appraisal and who does the choosing? Again we can look to the DES Circular for guidance:

▶ 'The appraiser is entitled to appraise performance across the full range of professional duties undertaken, including tempo-

rary responsibilities. Appraisal should be undertaken on the basis of an established job description.'

[Paragraph 19]

This takes us a little way forward, but only a little way. The appraiser is apparently entitled to choose the areas for appraisal. But it is an unwise appraiser who regards this as an absolute power. It is much better that the agenda should be set by a process of discussion and negotiation between the appraiser and the teacher, with a number of factors being taken into account.

Should there be any outside influence on this process? Should the headteacher, or another member of the management team, or even a governor or parent, be allowed to suggest areas where an individual teacher should be appraised? This is difficult territory. The answer with respect to governors or parents is almost certainly 'No'. They have no status in the detailed management of the school and any involvement in appraisal is likely to turn into a grinding of personal axes.

The question of senior management is different. Appraisal must not become a substitute for the proper function of management. Matters should not be referred to appraisal which are more appropriately addressed through the normal processes of management. However, an individual teacher may have a number of different roles, each managed by a different person: as classroom teacher, managed by the head of department; as personal tutor, managed by the head of year; as records of achievement coordinator, managed by the deputy head. Only one of these will be the teacher's actual line manager and, probably, appraiser. The other managers, and perhaps the headteacher as well, may think that there are issues which it would benefit both the school and the teacher to address during appraisal.

In these circumstances, it may well be legitimate for the head or another member of the management team to suggest agenda items to either the appraiser or, preferably, the teacher being appraised. But this should be the extent of the influence. The final decision must remain with the two partners in appraisal, for it is they who bear the responsibility for ensuring that appraisal can be carried forward in a positive manner, likely to be of benefit to both the teacher and the school.

The scope of the duties open to appraisal is set by the job description, and we will look more closely at the nature of job descriptions below. However, we still need criteria in order to select from within the job description. There are four criteria which we could use:

- the most important tasks;

- the most time-consuming tasks;

- the teacher's strongest areas;

- the teacher's weakest areas.

Each of these merits serious consideration. It is self-evident that the most important areas of a teacher's work should be appraised. It is on these areas that the quality of the teacher's work largely depends, and it is right therefore that it is these which should be put under the spotlight. The most time-consuming tasks may, of course, be the most important ones. Where this is not the case, these tasks perhaps merit examination – is the teacher spending too much time on work which is of low priority?

It is important that the appraisal process considers some areas where the teacher is strong. One of the purposes of appraisal is to confirm and celebrate good practice. Equally, however, weak areas need addressing so that the teacher can be offered proper professional support to overcome difficulties.

Ideally, the appraisal agenda should include items which satisfy each of the four criteria. Of course, discussion in these terms may be somewhat artificial. One item could actually satisfy up to three of the separate criteria. Further, it might be difficult for a teacher to identify strong and weak areas – that in itself may be one of the outcomes of the appraisal process.

In all this, we must take into account what the statutory regulations require. They direct that for all teachers except headteachers the appraiser shall observe the teacher teaching on at least two occasions. (Headteachers may be observed teaching or performing other duties.) Classroom performance must therefore form an item on the appraisal agenda of all teachers.

This requirement should not deter appraisers from focusing additionally on the management activities of senior and middle managers. Such managers will be receiving incentive allowances for their managerial responsibilities and they may spend only a small proportion of their time in the classroom. It is essential, both for the school and for the manager concerned, that appraisal should encompass these managerial tasks.

We shall look more closely in Chapter 11 at what the appraiser should actually observe when in the classroom. There are a number of issues to be taken into account when choosing which lessons or activities to observe. No-one is equally effective in all teaching situations. Teachers are often more proficient dealing with one age group rather than another, one ability group rather than another. They may be more comfortable with some teaching styles or learning activities. Their competence may vary according to the topic being considered. For example, a science teacher may be confident when dealing with biological aspects but may feel insecure with physical topics. Therefore, the choice of lessons for appraisal with respect to age, ability, activity or topic may critically affect what is observed and the apparent competence of the teacher.

When appraisal enters its second cycle, the agenda should take account of the areas appraised two years before. There seems little point in reappraising an area which was previously found to be perfectly satisfactory. It would be more productive if different areas and new concerns could be addressed.

▇ The job description

Appraisal should be firmly based on the teacher's job description. Unfortunately, for many teachers, that job description may be non-existent, or may be available only in a rudimentary form. When an appraisal system is being developed in a school, one of the first areas which may need attention is the creation or amendment of job descriptions. All teachers ought to be in possession of a clear job description which accurately reflects the duties and responsibilities laid on them.

What makes a good job description? Formats can vary, but the following are the essential contents:

1 The title of the post

2 The person(s) to whom the post holder is responsible

3 The objectives of the post

4 The areas in which the job will operate

5 The detailed duties associated with each area.

▇ 1 The title of the post

The title of a post is unlikely to give more than a flavour of what is actually involved. The title 'deputy head' in a secondary school usually gives only an indication of status in the hierarchy, not the specific duties undertaken. These will depend both on the number of deputy heads and on the division of responsibilities between the headteacher and the various deputies. In a primary school, the title 'science coordinator' denotes the teacher's management responsibilities, but fails to convey that the teacher is probably also carrying a very heavy teaching load.

■ 2 The person(s) to whom the post holder is responsible

When teachers have a number of duties in a number of different areas, they may well have different managers for the various responsibilities. The head of department may oversee classroom work, a head of year pastoral duties, a deputy head work as examinations secretary.

Sometimes the lines of responsibility may not be completely clear. The head may perhaps ask a teacher to take on new responsibilities, but may fail to designate a manager for the work. This can then lead to slack management. The teacher may be unsupervised, or may resent seeming interference from a member of the senior management team who in fact thinks that he or she has responsibility in this area.

Good management dictates that lines of responsibilities should be clearly defined, with just one line manager who bears overall responsibility for the teacher. If this is not the case, when appraisal begins, it may well be difficult to determine a suitable appraiser, to collect information, or to offer proper support for any difficulties which are detected during the appraisal process.

■ 3 The objectives of the post

The objectives will list succinctly, in summary form, the purposes for which the job exists. For instance, the job description of the staff development coordinator might include the objective:

'To establish and maintain a school policy for staff development and to create and coordinate a staff development programme.'

■ 4 The areas in which the job will operate

We have already noted that many teachers have a range of duties within and outside the classroom. For the purposes of the job description, it can be useful to divide these into generic areas, so that the range and the extent of the duties are clear.

Four general areas could be used:

- Teaching

- Pastoral care

- Staff management and administration

- External relations

Some teachers will have entries only under one heading, some under two or three, with perhaps only the most senior members in the hierarchy having entries under all four.

■ 5 The detailed duties associated with each area

The teacher's duties within each area should be listed under the appropriate heading. There is a question as to the degree of detail which should be employed. Teachers are professionals and should be allowed wide scope to use their flair and apply their qualities and skills in the ways which seems most appropriate to them. The job description should therefore leave ample discretion to the teacher.

The process through which a duty is converted into practice is as follows:

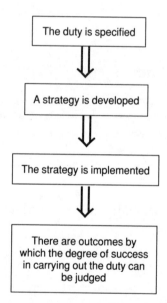

In general, only the duty will be specified in the job description. The teacher will then develop a strategy to carry out the duty, which will no doubt be discussed with the line manager. The teacher will also outline what he or she feels can be accomplished in this field and the hoped for outcomes.

At this stage the line manager will be able to comment on the appropriateness of the suggested strategies and the projected outcomes.

Changes to the strategies may be advised. Or revisions might be suggested to the proposed outcomes because they are not sufficiently challenging, or are indeed over-ambitious. In due course, the outcomes will
be used to judge the success of the teacher in carrying out the assigned
duty. Sometimes these outcomes will be the subject of appraisal.
Sometimes they will be looked at in the course of a normal management
review. What we are saying, however, is that it is inappropriate in a job
description to include either detailed goals or the means of reaching
those goals. The job description should confine itself to detailing the
areas in which the teacher will be working.

Thus, for instance, in a primary school, the science coordinator will
have listed under the heading 'management' a number of duties which
might include the following:

- to develop and maintain throughout the school a science curriculum which matches the requirements of the National Curriculum;

- to work with each class teacher to ensure the effective delivery of
  the agreed science curriculum.

It will then be a matter for discussion between the line manager and
the teacher as to how the responsibilities will be carried out in practice,
and over what time scale. These discussions will address many different
issues which will include, for instance:

- how the curriculum will be developed, and how other staff, outside advisors etc will be involved in the process;

- what staff development should be offered to the teachers in this
  area;

- what time and resources the teacher will have available – how
  much time can actually be spent with other teachers in their classrooms;

- how the success of the curriculum and its delivery will be evaluated – by teacher opinion, by pupil outcomes etc.

Thus the job description confines itself to the clear definition of the
tasks to be undertaken. This then forms a secure basis for the planning,
development and implementation of that work, for its monitoring and
support by the management team, and for its appraisal in due course
should that be appropriate.

9 Gathering evidence for appraisal

Evidence for appraisal

Evidence is crucial if the appraisal process is to be grounded in fact. Otherwise, appraisal becomes an exercise based on impressions, hearsay and prejudice. For the classroom teacher, by far the most important and most substantial source of evidence will be the periods of classroom observation. The net can, however, be spread wider than this and it becomes increasingly important to do so when the emphasis is on the duties of the teacher outside the classroom.

Sources from which evidence can be gathered include the following:

- the initial meeting;
- self-appraisal;
- classroom observation;
- other external evidence;
- pupil appraisal;
- pupil learning outcomes;

The first three of these are certainly the most important and we consider them in some detail in Chapters 10 and 11. The other sources we discuss here.

External evidence

Although classroom observation will produce the main evidence for the appraisal of classroom teachers, the appraiser may seek information on a broader spectrum. The statutory Regulations allow this, although 'not without first consulting the school teacher'. There is a Code of Practice laid down concerning the collection of information which we detailed in Chapter 5.

Why should the appraiser need this wider tranche of data? First, there may be a need for basic information. The appraiser may not, for instance, have a copy of the job description or the departmental aims. To some extent the amount of data required will depend upon the relationship of the appraiser to the teacher. In a primary school, the headteacher may be appraising a classroom teacher and may have immediate access to all the required documentation. In a secondary school, a teacher may have a number of roles in which he or she is not directly responsible to the line manager. In such cases, the line manager may need to gather background documentation together to gain more detailed data about these roles.

Second, there may be perceptions to be gathered from other 'witnesses'. Care must be taken in this region. It must not become a free for all, a gossip's charter. But, consider the situation where the teacher has responsibilities outside the classroom, for which the line manager does not bear immediate responsibility – a coordination role within the school, perhaps, or a pastoral role. There may then be others within the management structure whose observations will form valid evidence in the appraisal process.

Third, when the management tasks of senior and middle managers are being appraised, different forms of evidence may be required. For the staff development coordinator, planning documentation may be reviewed, and the range and style of development activities considered. A head of department may be observed chairing a departmental meeting, or the staff within the department may provide valid reflections about the way in which the department is being managed. If home-school liaison is a duty being appraised, then interviews with a sample of parents may give insights into the teacher's success in this field.

The greater the amount of data collected, the broader the perspective of the appraiser – and this will make the whole process more valid. However, there are some inherent dangers and difficulties. There is the whole ethical question: many teachers will feel uncomfortable about providing information about colleagues, particularly it if is in any way prejudicial. In a hierarchical situation, teachers may fear a come-back from their manager if they have expressed criticism to the appraiser. There may therefore be a lack of honesty in the process. Finally, such data gathering exercises are time consuming. The appraiser must be sure that the time spent in collecting information is justifiable in terms of improvement to the quality of the appraisal process.

▣ Pupil appraisal

Should pupils' opinions of their teacher be used as a source of data for teacher appraisal?

We now live in a market-driven environment where the customer is king. This influence is penetrating schools although in this context, it is the parent who is regarded as the customer, not the pupil. Of course, parents choose the school which their child will attend (in those areas where such choice is available). Even so, the child is often extremely influential in this decision, and the child's own perceptions are in turn influenced by reports from pupils already attending the schools under consideration.

Further, once children are attending a school, motivation is crucial to their learning. That motivation will often depend upon the feeling of partnership which the school creates and the sense of ownership of their own education which the children are allowed.

Given all these circumstances, it is strange that in many schools there is a reluctance to perceive the child as consumer. It is the child whose needs are being catered for, it is the child who receives the service which the school is offering. Many teachers will be actively seeking to develop the critical faculties of their students, whether those students are considering the environment, the media, art or advertising. Why should children be expected to suspend these same critical faculties when they are evaluating their own learning?

The reason is grounded in the hierarchical structure within a school, where pupils are at the bottom of the pile. Within hierarchies, criticism only goes downwards, not upwards. The teachers mutter in the staff room about the inadequacies of the senior management team. The children, similarly, are expected to confine their complaints to the playground. But increasingly, in the world of industry and commerce, hierarchies are breaking down. More lateral structures, with team building, are seen as more effective. Deference is disappearing. And the same influences are being felt in the staff structures of many schools.

Should the same facilities be extended to the pupils? Pupils obviously have perceptions about their teachers and about the learning being offered. Research suggests that these perceptions are quite valid, in both secondary and primary schools. Perhaps the question at the start of this section was wrongly phrased. The apposite question may be: 'Why should pupils' opinions of their teacher NOT be used as a source of data for teacher appraisal?'

■ Pupil learning outcomes

In discussing the collection of information, the National Steering Group Report states (paragraph 37) 'that there are other sources of information about a teacher's teaching which it may be appropriate to take into account, including the work and progress of children.'

Learning, in the broadest sense of the word, is what education is about. Learning outcomes are the evidence of learning having taken place. Some people would argue that learning outcomes are the most valid indicator of a teacher's competence. The methods used by a teacher are a means to an end. If the ends are satisfactory, then the means must be appropriate. Indeed, during the 1980s, from a point where teachers were being encouraged to adopt more enquiry-based, pupil-centred styles of learning, the emphasis switched to teachers using the systems with which they themselves could achieve the best results. Teachers, it was argued, should be aware of the repertoire of teaching/learning styles available, and most teachers would use a range of such styles. However, in the end it was a matter for the professional judgement of each individual teacher as to the methods which he or she chose to employ. That judgement would be evaluated against the pupil outcomes.

The problem with this approach is that it assumes that there is a precise, objective method of assessing those learning outcomes. It also begs the question, if the outcomes are good, whether they might have been even better had different strategies been adopted by the teacher.

Some would persuade us that National Curriculum Assessments, and GCSE at Key Stage 4, give us those objective measures. Should we therefore be seeing these assessment results as important evidence in the appraisal process?

National Curriculum assessment results will in future be published on a school-by-school basis. This data is intended to help parents and others to form a judgement about the standard of education prevailing in a particular school.

There has been much criticism of the publication of such data in a 'raw' form. It is argued that standards at the end of a Key Stage depend not only upon the teaching during that Key Stage, but also on the standards of the children at the beginning, together with their social and home background. In an inner city school, for instance, with a high proportion of pupils from homes where English is only a second language, teachers may do well in bringing the majority of pupils to level 1 in most attainment targets by the end of Key Stage 1. In another infant school, which draws pupils from highly literate homes, many pupils may be reaching level 3 at the end of Key Stage 1. The junior schools receiving these two cohorts of pupils at the beginning of Key Stage 2 will be starting from completely different base lines. It will therefore be inequitable to compare their results directly at the end of Key Stage 2.

On the other hand, it may be fair to compare the results on a 'value added' basis. In such a system, the level of the pupils at the beginning of the Key Stage is taken into account in evaluating the results at the end of the Key Stage. The crucial issue then becomes one of how much *progress* has been made over the intervening years.

The Audit Commission in Autumn 1991 published a Working Paper *Two Bs or Not ...?* A methodology is being developed to use GCSE as a basis for value-added judgements about post-16 education. In the research, GCSE grades were used as a base line to calculate the progress which pupils from different schools had made in different subjects by the time they took GCE A level examinations. It was found that it was not necessarily the schools with the highest A level grades in which students had made most progress. When the base line from which students started was taken into account, other schools progressed their students further, even though, because those students started from a lower base line, they did not achieve the highest A level grades.

The use of National Curriculum Assessment results to judge the competence of teachers raises the same issues. It would be unfair to use the raw results for several reasons. First, pupils entering a Key Stage will vary in their existing achievement. It is unreasonable to judge results at the end of the Key Stage without taking the initial starting point into account. Second, pupils are often taught by several different teachers during a Key Stage. The results at the end of a Key Stage will depend upon the competency of each of these teachers, not just the one in the last year of the Key Stage. Third, the desired outcomes from the course being offered may be only partially covered by the National Curriculum Assessment system. Whilst the National Curriculum will be at the core of what teachers are offering, teachers are likely to have additional aims and will be hoping to achieve other important outcomes.

National Curriculum assessment results will in due course constitute a useful tool for schools in their self-evaluation procedures. Schools will be able to compare their outcomes from subject to subject, from school to school, taking into account any external factors which may have affected those results.

As far as individual teachers are concerned, the use of National Curriculum results as evidence will be problematic. It is unlikely that assessment results will themselves be sufficiently sensitive to be acceptable as part of the appraisal evidence. For that to be possible, it would be necessary to ensure that pupils in each year of a Key Stage were reliably assessed in terms of National Curriculum levels, that there was a system in place to calculate the value added, and that the National Curriculum assessment validly reflected the outcomes which the teacher was seeking.

In conclusion, it may be thought best if pupil learning outcomes are looked at in the context of classroom observation. It is doubtful whether the external measures now available are sufficiently refined to be incorporated into appraisal evidence.

Criteria for assessing the evidence

Once the evidence has been gathered, it must be evaluated. Before discussing this process we must emphasise that evidence is gathered only as the basis for the appraisal discussion. It should not be used to form judgements about the teacher independent of those discussions. Appraisers will need to consider the quality of the evidence which has been collected; there are two aspects to this process: *validation* and *assessment*.

Validation

Appraisers first have to consider the validity of the evidence before them. Is it likely to be a fair representation of the teacher's qualities and competences? Are any external 'witnesses', whether other teachers, parents or pupils, reliable? Were the observed classroom sessions typical or atypical of the teacher's work?

Appraisers can use various processes in attempting to answer these questions. They can test one 'witness' against another, and against their own perceptions. They can test what the teacher says against the documentation provided and against what they observe in practice. They can compare the teacher's own opinions, expressed through self-appraisal, with the other evidence available. In the end, however, appraisers can only reach a personal judgement about the actual quality of the evidence before them. They must decide that which they can rely on most heavily, and that which is perhaps misleading in its nature.

Assessment

The evidence then has to be assessed, and for this criteria are necessary. This is a very difficult area, for there are few definitions of what constitutes good practice. What definitions there are tend to be general in nature. Perceptions about good practice also change.

Teachers have an intuitive feel for what works in their own classrooms. The best results are achieved when they employ the techniques with which they feel most secure. Methods imposed from outside, with which a teacher lacks confidence, can be doomed to disaster.

It would be wrong for appraisers to seek to impose their own perceptions of good practice. This will lead teachers merely to feel that the appraiser is offering another opinion which is neither more nor less valid than their own. As a prelude to appraisal, it may be possible for schools, or departments within schools, to develop a set of criteria for a 'good' lesson. This approach is no doubt a good staff development exercise and is invaluable in sharing professional ideas. But perfect prescription is unlikely to emerge, other than in a vague format, largely because any format has to be adaptable to the personality and skills of the individual teacher.

The answer may be to look not at the teaching process per se, but at the process in terms of outcomes. One then looks, not at what the teacher is doing in absolute terms, but what the teacher is doing in relation to the children. On this basis questions can start to be formulated.

- Is the lesson engaging the pupils?

- Do they understand the tasks, the materials?

- Are the needs of pupils of different abilities being catered for?

When the answer to questions such as these is 'Yes', we can judge the teaching process to be satisfactory, whatever methods may be used. When the answers are more equivocal, we then need to examine the teaching process in order to see how the outcomes may be improved. In Chapter 11, we list more detailed criteria in the form of questions which can be used during classroom observation. We commend a similar approach when the other forms of evidence are being considered.

10 Essential preparation? The initial meeting and self-appraisal

In the government's Regulations, there are two components of the appraisal cycle which are not compulsory: the initial meeting between teacher and appraiser, and self-appraisal. Nevertheless, we feel strongly that schools should consider them as essential elements in their appraisal procedures. In both cases, they are part of the preparations for the appraisal discussions and, as in many other situations, the importance of effective preparation is paramount.

The initial meeting

Throughout this book, we have tried to stress the importance of seeing appraisal as a genuinely two-way process between appraiser and teacher, and one which is carried out in a spirit of cooperation. In our view, the initial meeting plays a crucial role in developing that cooperative spirit, and sets the scene for all that follows. The meeting provides both parties with the opportunity to discuss how the appraisal will proceed, its scope, and what they expect it to achieve. The initial meeting should cover the following issues:

- the teacher's job description, and the degree to which it reflects accurately his or her work;
- the areas of the teacher's work on which the appraisal will focus;
- the information to be gathered;
- who will be involved in providing information;
- the number and length of classroom observations to be carried out;
- the timetable for the appraisal cycle.

■ Self-appraisal

Self-appraisal is not a compulsory element in the government's requirements for the appraisal of school teachers. However, there is a considerable volume of research evidence in favour of self-appraisal as an initial
part of the total appraisal process. We would recommend strongly that
schools include it in the procedures they draw up.

Self-appraisal can have a number of benefits, for the teacher, the
appraiser and the school. It can

- assist in making the appraisal a genuinely two-way process, particularly in the discussions of the teacher's performance, priorities
  and development needs;

- enable the teacher to clarify his or her perceptions and priorities;

- encourage the teacher to undertake regular reflection about his or
  her work and career;

- lead to greater commitment by the teacher towards the achievement of agreed targets;

- provide solutions to problems which are preventing the teacher
  from performing effectively.

Self-appraisal need not be seen as a formal exercise, nor as something
which only takes place as part of the appraisal process. Indeed, making
time to reflect on successes and failures, strengths and weaknesses, is to be
encouraged as a normal part of day-to-day professional life. Self-appraisal
can take a variety of forms, including:

- setting time aside for quiet reflection;

- writing about aspects of the job, and how successful each has been;

- identifying those aspects of the job which have been most successful and those which have been least successful;

- describing factors that help in achieving success, and those which
  inhibit or frustrate achievement;

- identifying personal development needs, both for the current job
  and for career aspirations;

- listing the various tasks involved in the job description and, for
  each, giving a rating for how well the task is going, for example on
  a 1 to 5 scale;

- evaluating success in achieving the targets set in the previous appraisal cycle.

Whatever form of self-appraisal is used, there are a number of issues to be considered. Teachers are often over-critical of their performance and, particularly, reluctant to praise themselves for their achievements and successes. This has much to do with teachers' self image; self-appraisal is likely to be much more positive in tone where the ethos of the school is one in which praise for good performance is a regular feature. This is particularly so in the day-to-day interactions between teacher and appraiser.

Some teachers will have shortcomings, or areas of their work which could be improved, of which they are unaware. Self-appraisal is unlikely to bring these to light. It will be an important role of the discussions between teacher and appraiser, both in the normal management relationship and in the appraisal process itself, to uncover such deficiencies. It is clearly helpful if such issues are raised at an early stage, so that the teacher can reflect on them before the appraisal discussion. The discussion will then provide an opportunity to explore the shortcomings and to compare the teacher's perspective with that of the appraiser and of any other teachers who have contributed information to the appraisal.

A further issue concerns the extent to which the teacher's self-appraisal is private. If the self-appraisal is to form part of the information for the appraisal discussion, the teacher may be reluctant to be totally honest about perceived shortcomings. This will be the case particularly if the teacher sees appraisal as directly linked to the possibility of disciplinary measures, promotion or pay. Equally, teachers' perceptions of how well they are doing in their jobs can provide a valuable – perhaps the most valuable – contribution to appraisal discussions.

One approach which may be helpful both in encouraging honest and rigorous self-appraisal and in providing valuable information for the appraisal discussion, is to have two self-appraisal documents. In the first, the teacher is encouraged to be honest and, where appropriate, self critical; this document remains private to the teacher, unless they wish to share it with the appraiser. The second document, which the teacher would produce specifically for the appraisal discussion, would contain only those aspects of the first document which the teacher is happy to provide for the appraiser.

It will be for each school to decide whether to include self-appraisal in its procedures and, if so, what form the self-appraisal should take, the guidance to be produced, and how the self-appraisal will be recorded. Where self-appraisal is to be a component of the appraisal cycle, some sort of standard self-appraisal form is likely to be of benefit to both the teacher and the appraiser. In designing self-appraisal forms, the following questions might be helpful.

Tasks and responsibilities

- What are the main tasks and responsibilities of your post?
- How do these compare with your current job description?
- Are there any tasks or responsibilities in your job description which you do not carry out?
- Are there any which are not in your job description which you think should be?

Success in achieving targets

- What were the targets set in your last appraisal?
- How well do you think you have done in achieving the targets?
- What helped you in achieving the targets?
- What prevented you achieving the targets in which you were unsuccessful?
- Were any of the targets inappropriate? If so, why?
- What targets might have been more appropriate?
- Overall, were the targets challenging, attainable and realistic?

Successes and failures

- Which parts of your job during the current appraisal cycle have been most successful?
- Have you received appropriate recognition for your achievements?
- Which have been least successful?
- What factors contributed to successes and to failures?

Job satisfaction

- Which parts of your job have given you the greatest satisfaction?
- Which have given you least satisfaction?
- How could these be made more satisfying?

Constraints

- Have there been any constraints on your work which have hindered you in carrying out your job?
- How might these be removed?
- What changes in the school's organisation would help to improve your performance?
- What additional things might be done by your headteacher? Your head of department? Other colleagues? You?

School and/or departmental development

- Which of the current developments in the school and/or your department most interest you?
- Would you like to be more involved in these? How?
- In what ways do you think the work of the school and/or your department could be improved?
- What contribution would you like to make to these improvements?

Targets

- What do you think should be your main targets for the next appraisal cycle?
- Which of these is your highest priority, and which is your lowest?
- What support will help you to achieve the targets?

Professional development

- What training or other development experience would help you to do your job better?

Career

- How would you like to see your career developing?
- In what areas do you need training, development or support to help you achieve the next step in your career?

11 Classroom observation

The observation of the teacher's work in the classroom will need to be handled sensitively. Many teachers are unused to being observed; the fact that the observation is part of the appraisal process may set up additional anxieties. To allay these anxieties as far as possible, it is important that both teacher and appraiser are clear about

- the purpose of the observation;
- what role the appraiser will play during the lesson;
- the criteria that will be used in observing the lesson.

Before the observation

Before any observation of classroom work, the teacher and observer should meet. While the government's Regulations state that the appraiser will observe the teacher teaching, we believe that there may be circumstances in which an alternative observer should be considered. For example, where a deputy head is appraising a teacher, it may be appropriate to agree that someone with greater knowledge of the teacher's subject will observe.

1 Which lesson?

The first thing to establish is which lesson is to be observed. Given the anxiety that the process may generate, it is probably sensible to allow the teacher to suggest which class should be observed and at what time in the school week – a particular class of pupils may react very differently depending on whether it is last lesson on Friday or first thing on Monday morning! While it is wise to allow the teacher to nominate the lesson to be observed, the observer can reserve the right to make the final choice, although this right will rarely need to be exercised.

In talking about the purpose of the observation, the observer should stress that it is intended to provide information for the appraisal process, rather than to make judgements about the teacher's ability. This should help to allay the teacher's anxiety, particularly about the validity of judgements made about such a small sample of teaching. It is helpful, too, to stress the partnership approach to lesson observation. In line with this approach, the pre-observation meeting should include discussion about the aims of the lesson, the teaching approaches to be used, the previous work on which the lesson will build and how the lesson will be followed up.

▉ 2 Focus of the observation

The opportunity should also be given for the teacher to suggest particular aspects of the lesson on which he or she would like the observer to focus. For example, the teacher might wish a particular focus on the teaching approaches used, or on the effectiveness of the arrangements for grouping the pupils, or on equal opportunities issues. The observer may also wish to suggest a particular focus, and the aspects which will be given special attention should be negotiated and agreed between the teacher and the observer.

▉ 3 Additional information

There should also be discussion about any additional information which would be useful to the observer in setting the lesson in context. Such information might include:

- samples of pupils' work;
- the teacher's planning notes;
- records of pupils' progress.

▉ 4 The observer in the classroom

The teacher will need to know what the observer will actually do while observing the lesson. This needs careful thought. On the one hand, the observer should aim to be as unobtrusive as possible. On the other, talking to pupils about their work can be the most effective way of finding out about what has been learned and pupils' attitude and motivation.

There are three points here. First, where visits to lessons by other teachers are a normal and accepted part of school life, even participative observation is unlikely to be disruptive to the work of the teacher and the pupils. Second, the observer needs to tailor what he or she does to what is going on in the classroom at the time. For example, it would clearly be a distraction (and bad manners!) for the observer to walk round the classroom, or to talk to pupils, while the teacher is attempting to talk to the whole class. On other occasions, for instance where the pupils are working on tasks individually, it will be possible to talk to pupils quietly about their work. Finally, there is the issue of taking notes and the form they will take. The use of any sort of checklist and, particularly, the use of clipboards will give the teacher and the pupils the clear impression that the teacher is being assessed. This practice should be strongly discouraged; it is far better to use a small notebook to make occasional notes as an aide memoire of significant aspects of teaching and learning.

▪ 5 What is 'good practice'?

The final issue on which the teacher and observer need to be clear is what is expected of the teacher in his or her work in the classroom; the criteria for 'good practice'. This is something that is best dealt with as a whole-school issues, rather than something to be decided between teacher and observer, although discussion and interpretation of the criteria to ensure common understanding may be valuable.

▪ Criteria for classroom practice

Producing criteria for classroom practice may be approached in a variety of ways. At one extreme, 'off the peg' sets of criteria from research writings or from the local authority can be used as they stand. At the other, meetings of the staff can be used to draw up criteria from scratch. The former has the advantage of saving time and effort, the latter of greater ownership and commitment on the part of teachers. A middle road may be best, taking established criteria as a starting point and involving the teaching staff in tailoring these to suit the school's particular needs.

As a starting point, it may be useful to consider the criteria used by the local authority in carrying out its inspections of schools. These should give clear evidence on what is looked for in teaching and learning, and may cover the following areas:

1 Content
2 Classroom management
3 Teaching approaches
4 Marking and assessment
5 Resources and display
6 Pupils' attitudes and behaviour
7 Pupils' work

Within each area, it is useful to draw up a series of questions or statements to act as a prompt list for the observer. Not all the questions below will be appropriate in every lesson.

---

1 Content

- Were the aims of the lesson clear?
- Was the content at the right level for the abilities and ages of the pupils?
- Were the activities which the pupils undertook relevant and set in context?
- Were the tasks and activities purposeful?
- Did the work take account of and build on pupils' previous experiences?
- Did the teacher set appropriate homework?

2 Classroom management

- Did the lesson have a clear beginning and a clear end?
- Were instructions given clearly?
- Did the teacher use praise and encouragement to reward good work and behaviour?
- Did the teacher have good control of the class?
- Was disciplinary action taken as appropriate?
- Did the teacher have high expectations of pupils' work and behaviour?

3 Teaching approaches

- Were the activities differentiated to take account of the differing abilities of the pupils?
- Was sufficient challenge provided for more able pupils?
- Were the activities provided for less able pupils within their capabilities?
- Did the teacher use a range of activities, and were these appropriate for the aims of the lesson and the abilities of the pupils?
- Did the teacher use questioning effectively, to make pupils think and to check their understanding?
- Did pupils have the opportunity to work cooperatively with others, in pairs or small groups?
- Was proper attention given to equal opportunities for all pupils?
- Were pupils encouraged to work independently, and to research or find things out for themselves?

4 Marking and assessment

- Was there evidence of regular marking of classwork and homework?
- Did the teacher make use of constructive comments and praise in assessing pupils' work?
- Did the teacher provide the pupils with feedback on their progress?
- Were records of pupils' work up to date?
- Were the criteria used to assess work clear and made known to the pupils?
- Were pupils encouraged to make assessments of their own work?

5 Resources and display

- Were the resources organised well and accessible to the pupils?
- Were the resources used appropriately for the tasks undertaken by the pupils?

- Did pupils have the opportunity to select the resources they needed for their work?

- Were there up-to-date displays of pupils' work and other materials?

- Did the displays cover a range and balance of pupils' work?

6 Pupils' attitudes and behaviour

- Were there good relationships between pupils, and between pupils and the teacher?

- Did pupils behave well?

- Were the pupils well motivated and interested in their work?

- Did pupils concentrate on their work?

7 Pupils' work

- Was pupils' work well presented?

- Was recorded work accurate, including spelling and punctuation?

- Did pupils demonstrate appropriate practical skills?

- Were pupils willing to discuss and ask questions?

- Did the pupils express themselves clearly and make use of a range of vocabulary?

Making use of the criteria used by the local authority in its inspection of schools, and amending them as appropriate, will serve a dual purpose: establishing what is expected of teachers for classroom observation as part of the appraisal process, and preparing the staff for future inspections of the school's work.

In addition to producing the criteria, the school needs to make sure that they will be understood and interpreted consistently. Involvement of all staff in the production of the criteria will certainly help in this, but the school might like to consider additional approaches, including:

- using a staff in-service day, or other training opportunities such as staff meetings, to discuss the meaning and interpretation of the criteria. It might be useful, in this context, to invite an inspector from the local authority to give a talk on how its criteria are used, or to lead the discussions.

- encouraging teachers working in the same department or, in primary schools, with pupils of the same or similar ages, to work together in the classroom. This will enable them to explore how the criteria work in practice and compare and resolve differences of interpretation.

- making opportunities for teachers from different departments, or teachers who teach different age ranges of pupils, to observe each other's lessons, to see how the criteria operate in areas with which they are unfamiliar.

Each of these approaches has implications for time and other resources, and will need to be considered in the context of the school's development priorities. Nevertheless, classroom observation is an important, and potentially threatening, part of the appraisal cycle, and it is important that criteria are understood and interpreted consistently.

■ Following the observation

Where possible, the observer should talk to the teacher immediately after the lesson to give his or her broad impressions of what took place; if it is not possible to do so immediately after the lesson, it should be as soon as possible thereafter. Teachers are usually keen to have immediate feedback, and delay may cause anxiety about what the observer's impressions might be.

After the observation, the observer should produce a summary of what took place, based on the brief notes taken during the lesson. This might be on a standard summary form, if the school has produced one as part of the agreed procedures. It is important not to leave this task for too long, in case the memory fades. Equally, some observers find it helpful to leave a day or so for reflection before writing a summary of the lesson. Having produced the summary, the observer may find it valuable to give a copy to the teacher. This will encourage the teacher to reflect on the observer's perceptions before the two meet to discuss more formally their perceptions of the lesson.

It is important that the formal meeting between the teacher and observer takes place as soon as possible after the lesson observation. The government's Circular recommends that this meeting should normally be within two working days of the observation. If the teacher is to have the opportunity to read and reflect on the observer's written summary of the lesson, this time scale may be unreasonable. Nevertheless, if the meeting does not take place within a week or so of the lesson, its value will be diminished, because both teacher's and observer's detailed recollection will be less sharp.

It is also important that the meeting is a two-way discussion. In addition to the feedback provided by the observer, there should be the opportunity for the teacher to give his or her impressions of how the lesson went, and how successful it was in achieving what was intended. The discussion should focus on the positive areas of the lesson, and any areas which were less impressive. The observer should not criticise the particular approaches used by the teacher, unless the outcomes in terms of pupils' learning were adversely affected by them. The teacher should also have an opportunity to describe any special circumstances which had an effect on the lesson, including the background and abilities of particular pupils.

If the discussion gives both teacher and observer the chance to give their perspectives on the lesson, and there is discussion and negotiation of any differences of view, an agreed summary of the lesson should be possible. This may be the summary produced by the observer, amended as necessary following the discussion. The summary should be signed by both to show that they agree that it is a fair record of the lesson. If there are unresolved disagreements, the teacher should append a note to the summary, giving details of the issues where views differed.

12 The appraisal discussion

The appraisal discussion is only one part of the appraisal cycle. It will probably last only for about one hour, and yet its success or otherwise will have a vital effect on the whole appraisal process and, beyond that, on the professional relationship between appraiser and teacher. A discussion which is positive, well run and skilfully handled will reinforce the mutual trust and confidence between teacher and appraiser, and will encourage a managerial relationship which both see as productive and helpful. Conversely, a discussion which is poorly organised, badly managed and negative in tone is likely to breed distrust and frustration, and may harm the future professional relationships between teacher and appraiser.

■ Purpose

The appraisal discussion has two major functions: to provide a formal opportunity to discuss the performance, aspirations, development and training needs of the teacher, and to agree targets for future action. In order to make the discussion as valuable and informative as possible, it should increase the amount of information about the teacher's work available to both the appraiser and the teacher. Information about the teacher's work can be divided into four categories, as shown in the diagram below.

	known to teacher	unknown to teacher
known to appraiser	Shared	Blind
unknown to appraiser	Private	Unknown

The information available to the appraiser and the teacher can be increased in two ways: through feedback provided by the appraiser; and through disclosure by the teacher of, for example, career aspirations or training needs. The increase in shared information is illustrated below.

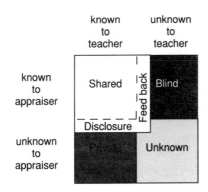

The appraisal discussion demands the application of a wide range of skills from both the appraiser and the teacher. These include:

- preparing;
- managing;
- providing feedback;
- listening;
- questioning;
- funnelling;
- summarising;
- setting targets.

Before considering these skills areas in detail, it is perhaps appropriate to lay down some guiding principles, within which these skills need to operate. The appraisal discussion should

- reinforce the mutual confidence and trust between teacher and appraiser. Nothing in the discussion should damage these essential aspects of appraisal.

- be positive. It should contain praise for good performance and suggestions for improvement for any areas of poor performance.

- focus on behaviour – what the teacher does and achieves – and not on personality – who the teacher is.

- look forwards rather than backwards. It is more helpful to consider ways in which performance may be improved than to concentrate on poor performance in the past.

- not be seen as an opportunity for dropping bombshells. Inadequate performance should be identified and dealt with in the normal processes of management.

- be carried out in a way which reflects the normal management style between the appraiser and the teacher. Where an appraiser would usually use a 'tell' style of management with the teacher – explaining, instructing, directing, indicating priorities – to approach the discussion in a 'participative' style – discussing, sharing ideas, negotiating – is likely to generate suspicion. Conversely, where the appraiser usually employs a participative or 'delegatory' style – authorising, trusting, giving power – an over-formal approach is likely to inhibit rather than encourage effective discussion.

■ Preparing

Our experience is that the appraisal discussion will not be successful unless both parties have prepared effectively. This involves:

- thinking;

- reflecting;

- reading.

Both teacher and appraiser need to give some thought to how they see the discussion going, what they will want to say, and what they want the process to achieve. Both, too, need to reflect on the teacher's performance, strengths and weaknesses, successes and failures. It is essential to make sure that all the essential documentation has been read and its implications considered. This will include the teacher's job description, the previous appraisal statement (including the targets agreed), notes on classroom observations, written comments from other teachers, and self-appraisal documents.

If this essential preparation is not carried out, time will be wasted in the discussion, sharing information which was already available to both appraiser and teacher, and one or both may leave the discussion with important issues not raised or intended outcomes not achieved.

■ Managing

It is the appraiser's responsibility to manage the appraisal discussion. This includes arrangements for the discussion, as well as the discussion itself. Arrangements involve:

- time;
- location.

The appraiser needs to ensure that there is sufficient time set aside for the discussion; it is unlikely that it can be carried out effectively in less than one hour. When it takes place is also important; last thing on a Friday afternoon, when both teacher and appraiser are tired and likely to be looking forward to the weekend, is unlikely to lead to a thoughtful and productive dialogue!

The location is also important. The appraiser needs to make sure that an appropriate room is booked for the discussion. The room needs to be warm, comfortable and airy – of course! – but, crucially, it must be private and free from disturbance. If there is a telephone in the room, it should be disconnected, where possible, or arrangements should be made to divert calls.

How the furniture in the room is arranged will also affect the discussion. Careful thought should be given to where the teacher and appraiser will sit. If the two chairs are directly opposite each other, and especially if there is a table or desk in between, the discussion may be steered towards a confrontational rather than a cooperative style. Equally, if the chairs are side by side, eye contact will be difficult. If the chairs are too close together, the teacher may feel oppressed or threatened; too far apart, and the discussion may lose its feeling of cooperation and professional sharing. One suggestion is to arrange the chairs and table as below.

One more thing: make sure that the chairs on which teacher and appraiser sit are of the same height. Chairs of unequal heights will do nothing to reinforce the feelings of participating in a discussion rather than in an interview.

The appraiser needs to have a clear idea of the structure of the discussion, and the approximate time to be spent on each item. Most discussions are likely to follow this structure:

- introduction;

- opening;

- discussing performance, including the teacher's perceptions and feedback from the appraiser;

- summarising;

- planning future action, including setting targets;

- closing.

It is important to remember that, even where the relationship is positive and friendly and where appraisal is viewed as a helpful and valuable process, the teacher is likely to be nervous and apprehensive. The appraiser should do his or her best to put the teacher at ease. It is best if the appraiser is already in the room, so that the teacher can be welcomed in a friendly and positive way. A question about family or how the teacher's day has gone might prove to be a useful ice-breaker. It is also necessary at this stage of the discussion for the appraiser to remind the teacher of why they are there, the purposes of the appraisal discussion, and the areas that they have agreed to discuss.

If the appraiser intends to take notes – and most will find it useful to do so – this should be explained to the teacher and carried out openly. Surreptitious note taking may lead to the teacher feeling that they are being assessed. Remember that the discussion should not be seen as judgemental!

Managing the pace of the discussion is another task for the appraiser. There will be a number of areas to be discussed, and sufficient time must be given to each. The appraiser needs to keep the discussion moving so that the agenda is covered, without rushing any item or getting bogged down in another.

The appraiser must try to ensure that the discussion ends appropriately. He or she should thank the teacher for contributing to the discussion and for giving up their time. It is a good idea, also, for the appraiser to say a few words about how the discussion went. Something like, 'thank you for being so positive. I found our discussion valuable and interesting – I hope you did too. I think the targets we agreed should be helpful. I look forward to hearing how you get on with them' will hopefully make the teacher feel that the time has been put to good use. A final task is to arrange a date for the review meeting, which takes place in the second year of the appraisal cycle.

■ Giving feedback

There are a number of general points which should be borne in mind when providing feedback. To be effective, feedback should

1 **Be immediate**. Managers should provide feedback on perfor-mance, whether positive or negative, as soon as possible. It should not be held back for the appraisal discussion. Remember that there should be no surprises! The appraisal discussion does, however, provide an opportunity to give feedback in a formal situation to reinforce that provided, perhaps, in more casual cir-cumstances. Saying, in the appraisal discussion 'You'll know how pleased I was with the way you dealt with that difficult situ-ation last week. But, I would like to repeat it this morning. Thank you.' is likely to be valued more highly by the teacher than a hur-ried 'Thank you for what you did yesterday' while meeting briefly at break time.

2 **Be positive**. Teachers receive insufficient praise for the good work they do, and this is not made better by the fact that many teachers find receiving praise rather embarrassing! Nevertheless, appraisers should take the opportunity of the appraisal interview to praise good performance. Even where performance is less than satisfactory, expressing feedback in pos-itive terms, describing what the teacher might do to improve performance, rather than concentrating on the poor performance itself, is likely to be received positively as well.

3 **Be specific**. It is much more helpful to the teacher to say 'I thought that talk you gave to parents last week on the National Curriculum for English was excellent' than 'You talk well to groups of adults.' Similarly, 'I think you might have dealt rather more firmly with that girl who was behaving unacceptably in your class yesterday' is more likely to lead to positive discus-sions about the strategies to deal with such situations than 'I'm worried about your classroom management'.

4 **Be based on evidence**. Describe things that have happened, and on which you have direct evidence, rather than making general

and unsubstantiated statements. Providing opinion as fact should also be avoided. Of course, the professional judgement of the appraiser is an acceptable, indeed valuable, part of the appraisal discussion. But where the appraiser is making a judgement, that should be made clear. It is better, for example, to say 'In my view, you didn't deal with that situation as well as you might have done', than 'You handled that badly'.

5   **Avoid gossip**. It is important to avoid statements which begin 'Some of your colleagues feel that …' or 'I hear that you …'. It is an essential part of successful appraisal that the whole process should be open and professional. The Code of Practice in the Government's Circular on appraisal is quite clear on this issue: 'Any information received anonymously should not be used' and 'Those giving information should be encouraged to make fair and considered comments which they are prepared to acknowledge and to substantiate if required'.

6   **Be descriptive**, rather than evaluative. It is better to describe poor performance, for example, than to draw general conclusions from what is observed. 'You lost control of that class' may be appropriate; 'You can't control classes' is not.

7   Above all, be **fair and honest**. The appraisal relationship is based on mutual trust and confidence. If trust is to be maintained, the teacher needs to be sure that the appraiser will provide fair, honest feedback. We must always remind ourselves that appraisal is all about maintaining and improving professional performance. If there is evidence of weakness in an area of a teacher's work, it is just as important that the appraiser gives full and honest feedback about this area of work, as it is about areas where performance is good. It would be very unfair to the teacher not to do so; how can improvement be expected until the area of weakness has been identified, and strategies for improvement discussed?

Appraisers often ask if it is better to give any negative feedback at the beginning, so that it is got out of the way quickly. This is almost certainly the wrong approach. The teacher is much more likely to respond positively to criticism of poor performance in one area, if he or she has previously received justified praise in another.

A final point that is worth making is that *how* something is said in feedback is often as important as *what* is said. If appraisers use a patronising tone when praising good performance, or give an impression of insincerity, then the effect on the teacher is likely to be less positive than if no praise were given at all.

■ Listening

It may be obvious that appraisers need to listen. Of course it is, but two questions need to be addressed: 'How much listening?' and 'What sort of listening?'. The answer to the first of these is probably 'as much as possible'. Precise percentages are not possible, but the appraiser should probably aim to talk for 20–30% of the time and the teacher, consequently, for 70–80% of the time. You may ask why this should be the case, given that the appraisal discussion is a dialogue between two professionals. We must remember that the appraisal is of the *teacher's* performance, and not of the appraiser's. It is important, therefore, that the person whose work is being appraised, and who will need to act on the agreed targets, does the lion's share of the talking.

There are different ways of listening. First, there is what we might call *party listening*; in casual conversation, we will often only half listen, making encouraging noises at what seem like appropriate junctions. On the other hand, there is what we might call *waiting listening*, where the listener is simply (and often obviously!) waiting for a gap in the conversation to make his or her contribution to the discussion. Neither of these sorts of listening is appropriate for the appraisal discussion. The sort of listening we require here is much more difficult. it can be described as *active listening*. This involves listening carefully to what is said, listening particularly for key words, thinking about what is being said, its implications and consequences, and using what is said to develop the discussion.

Effective listening is a difficult skill and, like the other skills in this chapter, needs practice to develop and master. Teachers are usually good communicators but, often, their talking skills are rather more developed than their listening skills!

Even where the appraiser is listening effectively, other factors can get in the way. In particular, *non-verbal signals* can be influential in the impression given by the appraiser. As well as listening, it is important to be *seen* to be listening. This involves showing that you are interested in what is being said, and this will usually show on your face. Maintain appropriate eye contact – but don't stare – and change your expression in response to what is said. Try to avoid signals which give the impression of lack of interest, such as yawning, looking at your watch, or out of the window, or which are likely to distract the speaker, such as frowning or tapping the table. When talking, it is equally important to look for signals in the person who is listening to you. Look and listen for signs of impatience, distress or disagreement and react accordingly.

■ Questioning

As important as listening well is the skill of asking the right questions. Remember that the purpose of the discussion is to increase the amount of information available to the teacher and the appraiser; questioning is the skill which will encourage and enable the teacher to reveal information to the appraiser. There are different sorts of questions; some are appropriate in some situations and not in others. Remember also that nothing in the discussion should damage the mutual trust between teacher and appraiser; the questions asked will be an important factor here.

There are some sorts of questions which should be avoided. These include *unprofessional questions, leading questions* and *multiple questions*. In the first category are questions like these: 'Don't you think that Mr Smith is rather ineffective in his role as head of year?', 'How do you spend your time at weekends?' and 'Don't you think your personal life is distracting you from your work at school?'. Leading questions are not improper in the same sort of way, but they are rarely useful in an appraisal discussion. A question like 'I'm sure you agree that you ought to change the way you teach?' is, first of all, judgemental. Second, it will give the teacher the impression that the appraiser is forcing his or her own view. The result is likely to be much more effective if the appraiser, through honest feedback and skilful questioning, can give the teacher the opportunity to come to the same conclusion.

Multiple questions consist of questions such as: 'What help are you providing to others in your role as technology coordinator, and how is that affecting your own classroom performance?' They are bad practice because they complicate matters unnecessarily; they require the listener to keep many parts of the question in mind and to decide on an answer to each. Quite simply, it is better to break such a complex question into single questions.

Closed questions can be useful to obtain specific information. A question like 'Have you suggested that idea to the headteacher?' is a closed question – it is likely to get a yes or no response – but may yield useful information quickly. Closed questions should not be overdone, or the discussion will yield a series of monosyllabic answers, and the result will be much closer to a rapid-fire quiz than a genuine professional dialogue!

The sorts of questions which are of greatest value are those which encourage the release of information, lead to shared understanding, or stimulate thinking about future action. We can categorise these as:

- open questions;
- reflective questions;

- hypothetical questions;
- probing questions.

Open questions permit a wide range of responses and encourage the appraisee to expand on ideas. A closed question such as 'Was the standard of work in that class high because it was a top set?' may well lead to a yes or no response, whereas 'How do you explain the high standard of work in that class?' is more likely lead to a considered and extended answer.

Reflective questions involve reflecting back to the teacher the words or ideas they have used in response to a question. They are used for checking understanding. They often begin with 'What exactly do you mean by ....?' Simply repeating a key word or phrase may achieve the same effect. For example, a teacher might say 'I've been finding the pupils hard going recently'. A reflective question here might be 'Hard going?' or 'Recently?'. depending on which of the key parts of the statement the appraiser wishes to have clarified. The former question will encourage clarification of what the teacher means by hard going or the pupils' behaviour that makes it so, while the latter will lead to an explanation of the time period the teacher is talking about.

Hypothetical questions are a way of getting the teacher's reactions to possible future actions. The appraiser might ask, for example, 'If you were to take on responsibility for coordinating the department's work in the sixth form, how would you approach the task?' or 'If we were able to send you on a course to acquire skills in information technology, what might be the benefits for the school?' The advantages of expressing such ideas in the form of questions, rather than statements like 'I'd like you to take on responsibility for sixth form work', or 'I think you should go on a course to improve your information technology skills' are the encouragement of a cooperative approach to decision making and the opportunity for the teacher to identify the benefits, difficulties and consequences of the suggested actions.

Probing questions can be used to get more information or to help move the discussion from the general to the particular. For example, the teacher might say 'I'd like to make a greater contribution to the work of the department.' A suitable probing question might then be 'What are the particular areas that you'd like to be involved in?' Again, in terms of career development, the teacher might say 'I think I'd like to apply for deputy head teacher posts'. Appropriate probing questions might be 'Are there any areas of the deputy headteacher's role that you would need to develop?' or 'In what ways can I help?'

■ Funnelling

The skills of listening and questioning do not work in isolation. The skilful appraiser combines active listening and the use of the various types of question we have described above to shape the discussion and to lead from the general to the specific, so that summarising and target setting are made easier. We call this process *funnelling*. A funnelling sequence in a discussion might follow this pattern:

- ask an open question;
- listen;
- use a reflective question to check understanding;
- listen and pick up key words in the response;
- use a probing question to get more detailed information;
- listen;
- use a reflective question to check understanding;
- listen;
- use a hypothetical question to explore a possible way forward;
- listen;
- summarise, and check that the teacher agrees with the summary;
- agree a target for action.

You will see in this sequence just how significant a role listening, particularly active listening, plays in the funnelling process. Quite simply, unless the appraiser listens effectively, he or she is unlikely to know which questions are the ones which will funnel the discussion towards the nub of an issue and lead to appropriate and helpful targets for action.

■ Summarising

The discussion of the teacher's work and performance will cover a number of key areas, which will have been agreed by the appraiser and the teacher at their initial meeting. To make the setting of targets at the end of the discussion easier to manage, it is useful to summarise what has been said at the end of each key area and to flag areas in which targets might be developed.

One important task that summarising can achieve is the avoidance of misunderstanding; it provides an opportunity to voice the appraiser's perceptions of what has been said and for the teacher to add his or her own comments and to resolve any disagreements. To encourage the teacher to contribute to the summarising process, it is often helpful for the appraiser to express the summary in the form of a question. Following a discussion about the teacher's role as a form tutor, for example, the appraiser might say, 'So, John, to sum up on your work as a form tutor, is what you're saying that you are pleased with the relationships with most of the pupils, but that one particular girl seems disaffected and uncooperative and that you'd like some guidance about how to deal with her?'

After the teacher has had the opportunity to confirm, amend or add to what has been suggested, it may also be useful for the appraiser to indicate that he or she would like to return to this issue at the end of the discussion.

Something like 'Perhaps we can come back to this after we've discussed other aspects of your work. It might well be an area where we can agree on a target for next year'. A brief note of the agreed summary of this aspect of work and the possibility of producing a target relating to it might be useful at this point, before moving on to the next area.

When all the agreed areas for discussion have been covered, the appraiser should then provide an overall summary, drawing on the notes of the summaries for each area. Again, the opportunity should be given to the teacher to confirm or add to the summary. This agreed summary will form the basis of the appraisal statement. So long as the teacher has been given the opportunity to contribute to the summary, the possibility of disagreement about the appraisal statement should be greatly reduced.

We will look at the final appraisal discussion skill, setting targets, in detail in the next chapter.

13 Target setting and review; and professional development needs

Part of the function of the appraisal discussion is to set targets for the remainder of the appraisal cycle. In this chapter we shall look at the purpose of targets, the ways in which they can be set, and the process of monitoring and review.

■ The purpose of setting targets

Appraisal should be a forward-looking process. Its initial focus is current practice – observed in the classroom and through other evidence, and reviewed during the appraisal discussion. The purpose of this review, however, should be developmental in nature. It is not undertaken in a summative sense, 'to find out how good the teacher is' nor yet in a critical sense, 'to find out how bad the teacher is'. Its purpose is to evaluate where the teacher is now so that this base can be built on to the benefit of the pupils, the individual teacher and the school as a whole.

Appraisal per se is a passive process. It identifies strengths and weaknesses. Target setting actually moves appraisal from the passive into the active. It is the process of deciding how we go forward from the present base and in which directions. It defines our future goals.

Target setting can be viewed as establishing an action plan for improving professional practice. The action plan will lay down what it is we wish to achieve, how and when it will be achieved, and how we shall know when it has been achieved.

Targets are first of all part of the teacher's own personal development plan. They express the directions in which he or she wishes to move, they reflect the issues which are seen as being of greatest importance. It is essential therefore that teachers should take an active part in the target setting process so that they are fully committed to these goals. The goals themselves, and the act of striving to meet them, will then act as a powerful motivator in the period ahead.

Targets cannot, however, just be part of a personal development process. They must also form part of the school development process. The school has its own aims and objectives, and the school development plan is the means by which these are progressively implemented. As far as possible, therefore, each teacher's targets need to be set within overall school policies. Sometimes the policies will arise from initiatives within the school – a decision to improve the pastoral system, for instance, or to develop cross curricular work. Sometimes they may arise from external imperatives – the need to introduce the National Curriculum, for example.

Target setting therefore has enormous potential for setting teachers' personal action plans within an action plan for the whole school. The effect is then to coordinate the efforts of the whole staff towards common goals. The role of the appraiser is crucial in creating the link. The appraiser should have a picture of the school's overall goals and should work to motivate the teacher towards pursuing these, so that the connection is made between the teacher's own aims and those of the school. The teacher is then happy to develop a personal action plan which is harnessed to the school development plan. This will obviously be easiest when the school development plan has grown out of whole staff discussion and action. If individuals already have ownership of the school's overall targets, they will have no difficulty in linking their own into these.

■ Setting the targets

A target is a specification of the action required to achieve an agreed priority in the teacher's work. It might relate to improvement in a particular aspect of performance, to a task to be undertaken, to participation in a team activity or project, to a whole school development, or to an aspect of professional development.

We have said above that the teacher is integral to the target-setting process. The role of the appraiser should be to help the teacher to identify targets, rather than to impose his or her own views of what those targets should be. Targets are much more likely to be achieved and to lead to genuine professional development if the teacher has suggested them and is convinced of their value. In helping the teacher to arrive at a set of targets for action, the appraiser can

- take advantage of ideas from the teacher. These might have arisen in the appraisal discussion itself, or through the day-to-day management relationship between the teacher and appraiser. Listening and questioning skills can be used to explore these suggestions, including the reasons behind them, their advantages and disadvantages, and how they might contribute to the teacher's performance and professional development.

- draw out other suggestions from the teacher. It may be possible to enable the teacher to come up with alternative targets to the ones which were suggested originally, which are more realistic, or more challenging, or which fit better with the teacher's professional development. For instance, the appraiser might ask: 'Are there other ways in which you could achieve the same result?'

- put forward a number of alternative suggestions. These can be phrased using hypothetical questions so that the discussion can explore the advantages and disadvantages of each. There may, perhaps, be a target which would be appropriate for the teacher and which fits in with the needs of the school.

At times, the process will call for great skill and patience from the appraiser. The targets which 'emerge' should be challenging, yet attainable, and should address the needs both of the teacher and of the school. Not all teachers will immediately see their way clear to setting such targets.

There are three main areas which should be considered for target setting:

1 The teacher's work in the classroom

Targets might then be involved with:

- the **curriculum** – the development of new curriculum materials;

- **pedagogy** – the introduction of a more varied teaching style or the use of a wider range of learning resources;

- **classroom management** – a change in the way resources are arranged or pupils are grouped;

- **pupil outcomes** – looking for improvements in certain curriculum areas or with particular groups of children.

2 The work of the school, or of the department

Targets will then be directed towards areas where the school as a whole (or the department) is trying to raise its performance – perhaps the development of a new record keeping system, or the introduction of records of achievement, or the coordination of skills across the curriculum.

■ 3 The teacher's personal development

The teacher might decide to take on a new management responsibility within the school, or to broaden his or her knowledge and expertise in a particular curriculum area.

In considering target setting, there are seven questions to be answered:

1 How many?

2 How quickly?

3 How difficult?

4 How precise?

5 How assessable?

6 How subject to change?

7 With what resources?

■ 1 How many?

Targets are not concerned with the day-to-day completion of a teacher's normal work. 'To complete the duties laid down within the job description' is not a target. Targets are about improvement. Therefore, just as appraisal cannot efficiently sample all the areas of a teacher's work, so it would be a mistake to seek improvements in too many areas. The effort required from the teacher should be realistic, taking into account the fact that achievement must also be maintained in the other aspects of the post.

The number of targets should therefore be limited – between two and five probably gives an optimum number. This means that there will have to be some prioritising in target setting, and it may be a matter of balance. Sometimes the priority will be improvement in a particular aspect of the teacher's work; sometimes it will be the need of the school as a whole to raise the quality of what it offers in a given area.

Targets may vary in size. Some could be major: 'To review the available primary mathematics schemes, with a view to recommending a new whole-school policy'. Some could be more routine: 'To ensure that marking is kept up to date'. The size of each target set, and the time which it will take to accomplish, will obviously affect the overall number specified.

■ 2 How quickly?

Appraisal takes place over a two year cycle. In some ways this is inconvenient from the teaching point of view, since much of the planning is matched to the academic year. Annual targets might therefore seem to make more sense.

In fact, there may be a natural timescale associated with particular targets. Some can start immediately – keeping marking up to date, for instance. For some, the span of a term might be appropriate. Others might take a year to complete. Exceptionally, targets may stretch even further into the future. There is an advantage in having different time spans. If all targets have the same time frame, the teacher may run into difficulties as the deadline approaches. Thus targets might best be a combination of shorter and longer term tasks.

■ 3 How difficult?

It is important to ensure that targets are achievable. Most teachers are already heavily burdened and the imposition of additional targets should not make their task impossible. There is therefore a balance to be struck. On the one hand, targets must not be too low level, too easily accomplished. They must provide a challenge. They must stretch the person concerned and bring about real professional development or improvement in performance. On the other hand, they must be sensible in terms of the time available and the improvement which can reasonably be expected. If over-ambitious targets are set, they can only result in failure, with a consequent demotivation of the teacher concerned.

It is the appraiser's job to preserve this balance as targets are negotiated with the teacher. Some teachers will no doubt be seeking an easy life and be looking to settle for low level, trivial tasks. More often, however, the appraiser is likely to have to save teachers from being too exacting and from setting targets outside the realms of possibility.

■ 4 How precise?

Targets should be

- specific;

- assessable;
- attainable;
- relevant;
- time-related.

Teachers should take away from their appraisal discussion a set of targets which tell them what they are expected to achieve and over what timescale.

■ 5 How assessable?

If the target setting process is to be effective, both the teacher and the appraiser must be able to judge when a target has been achieved. Each target must therefore be assessable. Ideally, the criteria by which it is to be assessed should be made explicit during the appraisal discussion. Thus the teacher will know at the beginning exactly what he or she needs to do.

This does not mean that targets will be measurable in any quantifiable sense. Very few targets will give rise to numerical performance indicators. Rather, there will have to be a professional assessment of the change which has taken place. The target might be, for instance, 'To improve classroom management'. This target on its own would not be sufficient. The appraiser and teacher would need to explore the ways in which the teacher's management should be improved, the support which the teacher would be given to facilitate this development, and the consequent changes which would be looked for in pupil learning or behaviour. In effect a detailed agenda for change would have been set and this would form the basis for review at a later date.

Targets which do not allow for such professional assessment are unsatisfactory in nature. By definition, they do not give a clear picture of the change required, and they are therefore too indefinite for inclusion in the appraisal process.

■ 6 How subject to change?

Change and innovation in education are taking place at a frenetic pace. The timescale allowed by the government for the implementation of its initiatives is often extremely short. The picture at the end of a two-year appraisal period might be completely different from that at the beginning.

In these circumstances, it would be wrong to regard targets as being cast in concrete. Events either within or outside the school may effect a substantial shift in priorities. Teachers' efforts may have to be refocussed at short notice. However, if a change of targets is necessary, it should be negotiated according to an agreed procedure. Teachers should not, on their own initiative, be allowed to lay aside agreed targets; nor should changing circumstances be used as an excuse by a teacher at review for the non-fulfilment of targets. When change is necessary, there should be a meeting between the appraiser and the teacher to explore the new circumstances, and to come to a redefinition of the agreed targets. In a constantly changing environment, the system must be flexible; it should not be open to abuse.

Teachers may also find during the development period that there are constraints to their meeting the agreed targets. The support which they were promised might not have materialized; anticipated resources might not be available. These are legitimate reasons for looking again at the targets and modifying them in accordance with the new circumstances. It is useful however if potential constraints can be considered during the appraisal discussion itself so that contingency plans can be laid – 'if ... this happens, then ... we will do this'. Such anticipation can make the whole process run much more freely.

▓ 7 With what resources?

The question of resources must be considered in relation to target setting. Targets can only be set within the limits of available means. Any reallocation has to be considered in terms of cost-effectiveness and the effect on other teachers or aspects of school life.

The appraiser must therefore beware of targets which depend for their realization on the commitment of additional resources. Promises must not be given which cannot be fulfilled. Where the resources are within the control of the appraiser, perhaps when heads of department are appraising members of their own department, there may be no problem. When resources are not under the jurisdiction of the appraiser, there could be greater difficulties. Some targets will depend upon additional resources – human or material, or outside support – training or consultancy. In these circumstances, it is wise either to specify alternative targets or to make contingency plans should the necessary resources not be realised.

▓ A checklist for target setting

Whatever targets are agreed, it is important that, at the end of the appraisal discussion, both teacher and appraiser should be completely clear about

- what the teacher is expected to do;
- the date by which the target should be achieved;
- who else will need to be involved;
- what support, training and resources will be needed to help the teacher to achieve the target;
- what will indicate that the target has been reached;
- how progress will be monitored.

As an illustration of how this might work in practice, consider the following target for the head of the English department in a secondary school.

Target	To produce guidelines for the use of information technology in English.
Deadline	End of the current academic year.
Others involved	Members of the English department, the school's IT coordinator, deputy headteacher.
Resources, training etc	Use of a staff in-service day for training for all members of the English department led by the IT coordinator; attendance at an LEA in-service training course by the second in department (two day course).
Performance criterion	Existence of guidelines document.
Monitoring	Half termly meetings with deputy headteacher to review progress (dates to be arranged).

To summarise, there are a number of ground rules for agreeing a set of targets in the appraisal discussion. Targets should

- be related to the needs of the teacher;
- facilitate the professional development of the teacher;
- be linked to the school development plan;
- be relatively few in number – four or five at most;
- be challenging;

- be realistic in scope;
- be attainable;
- be expressed as actions and results, not as processes;
- be specific, clear and unambiguous;
- have deadlines for their achievement;
- be achievable within available resources;
- be assessable;
- have clear criteria for success;
- be subject to regular, prearranged monitoring;
- be subject to change when there is a substantial shift in priorities.

■ Meeting professional development needs

The appraisal process will almost certainly identify areas in which the teacher can develop and improve. The teacher may respond positively to the idea. The question then arises as to how change can be brought about. It is not a matter just of willing the ends.

The appraisal system itself will help because participation in the actual process will develop in teachers the qualities and skills required to gain insights into their own practice. However, most teachers will also need a positive programme of support if improvement is to become a reality. Appraisal should not stop at the point of defect identification. It must also formulate the solution – or at least the means to the solution. Thus a discussion of the individual teacher's perceived future development needs is integral to the appraisal process. Satisfying those development needs for all teachers is a challenge for the school's management.

Traditionally, schools have met the professional development needs of individual teachers by arranging for them to attend specific training events, often organised by the local education authority's advisory service, universities or other providers. A number of factors now make this approach less automatic.

First, changes in the funding arrangements for in-service training courses some years ago mean that secondments and extended training courses funded by local authorities are now relatively rare.

Second, most local authorities now delegate to schools a substantial proportion of the money for in-service training, which was previously held centrally. Instead of having a range of courses which teachers could attend at no cost to the school, funds are provided to the school, and it can use these to pay for courses attended by teachers or to spend on other in-service activities.

Third, the introduction of staff in-service days as part of the Teachers' Pay and Conditions Act 1987 has led to an increase in the amount of school-based training.

There are two further factors, concerned more with the effect on schools, rather than with the availability of courses or funding. It has become increasingly difficult in schools to arrange for appropriate supply teachers to cover for teachers attending courses. There is also unease among headteachers, governors and parents about the effect on the teaching and learning of pupils of large numbers of absences of teachers attending in-service courses.

In its report *Developing School Management: the way forward*, the School Management Task Force recommended a shift in the emphasis from attendance at courses to school-based and school-focused training. Some attendance at courses will still be necessary and desirable, for instance on aspects of the National Curriculum, but the emphasis should be on training and development which takes place within the school, and which relates to the needs of the institution as well as to those of the individual teacher.

Development opportunities which can be provided within the school include:

- team teaching;
- job shadowing;
- observing teachers in other classrooms;
- taking on responsibility for an aspect of school development;
- joining or leading a working group looking at a particular aspect of school development;
- exchanging responsibilities with another teacher;
- temporary responsibilities;
- carrying out a piece of research;
- evaluating a school development;
- producing guidelines, policies or schemes of work;
- acting as a mentor for new or less experienced colleagues;
- leading or taking part in school-based training;

- receiving individualized advice and counselling from a member of staff within the school or from an outside adviser;

- discussion within self-help groups within the school or within consortia of schools;

- undertaking a schedule of planned reading.

Appraisal should therefore result in an individualized training and development programme for each member of staff. Such programmes will of course need to be prepared within the resources available. Appraisers should be wary of establishing targets which will demand excessive training resources, or of making promises of support which the school is unlikely to be able to meet. Such action can only result in disappointment, and eventual demotivation, for the teacher.

Professional development programmes arising from appraisal should be coordinated within the school's overall staff development policy. Headteachers can then ensure, as is required of them by the 1987 Conditions of Service, that they have a staff development policy 'which as far as possible caters for the training and development needs of the individual within the context of the school's overall needs and priorities'.

■ The process of monitoring and review

The second year of the appraisal cycle is devoted to following up the targets set in the appraisal discussion and, specifically, to the review meeting. When targets are set during the appraisal discussion, and included in the appraisal statement, this implies commitment by both teacher and appraiser to ensure that the targets are achieved. We will discuss below the role of the formal review meeting, but it is important to understand that the meeting itself will not be sufficient to ensure that targets are achieved. Rather, follow-up needs to be seen as a continuous process to which both appraiser and teacher must contribute.

In addition to the review meeting, it may be useful to arrange periodic meetings to check on progress in achieving targets, to identify any factors which are preventing success, and to establish what specific support the appraiser or others within the school can provide to help the teacher achieve the targets. Equally important is the day-to-day support which the appraiser can provide in giving encouragement, sustaining morale and showing interest in developments. For his or her part, the teacher must be prepared to keep the appraiser informed of progress made and any help required. In short, openness about what is happening, and a supportive ethos, are needed for both teacher and appraiser.

◼ The review meeting

The review meeting is the formal opportunity to exchange information about how the teacher is faring in achieving the targets agreed in the first year of the appraisal cycle. If the day-to-day contact between appraiser and teacher has been maintained, as suggested in the previous paragraph, then the meeting should contain no surprises; both will be aware of which targets are going well and which not so well.

The review meeting should consider the following:

- progress made in achieving each target;
- whether the targets are still appropriate and whether they need to be modified in the light of changing circumstances;
- evaluation of any training which has been undertaken, and the outcomes expected of any future training;
- any particular issues about the teacher's work;
- career development needs.

As soon as possible after the meeting, the following should be recorded on the appraisal statement:

- the fact that the meeting has taken place;
- any agreed modifications to targets;
- the reasons for such changes.

◼ Conclusions

Target setting can have a number of benefits:

1 It can improve teachers' performance.

2 It can lead to a focusing of priorities.

3 It can increase efficiency by concentrating teachers' attention on the most important aspects of their work.

4 It can help to coordinate teachers' efforts across the school and align them to school policy.

5 It can improve teachers' motivation.

6 It can improve teachers' self-awareness.

7 It can improve teachers' morale.

14 Training for appraisal

The national picture

The Report of the National Steering Group emphasized the importance of training for appraisal:

▶ **'73. Training is essential if teachers and headteachers are to be able to operate appraisal schemes in a manner which will help to improve the effectiveness of schools . . . Several important points emerged from the (pilot) study, including the need to provide adequate training for appraisees as well as appraisers; the benefits which flow from giving each an insight into the other's role; the benefits of simulated role playing, for example, mock appraisal interviews; and the need to plan training so that it takes place as near to the actual experience of appraisal as possible.'**

Properly handled, appraisal will be welcomed by teachers as an additional aid to their professional competence and development. For these positive benefits to be reaped, however, it will be essential for schools to develop an effective training strategy and to mount a professional training programme.

Developing a school policy for training

The LEA is the appraising body for all maintained schools. As such, it will be responsible for all aspects of appraisal set out in the regulations. As part of this supervisory role, most LEAs will see themselves as having a role in training. At the very least, this will include bidding for the government funding which is available for appraisal training. Most LEAs will no doubt be able to mount comprehensive and supportive training programmes throughout the whole introductory phase. Other LEAs may find it necessary to delegate much of this responsibility to the individual schools.

Whatever the support received from its LEA, however, the school has a clear responsibility to develop its own training strategy for appraisal and to incorporate this into the school development plan and staff development policy. Proper coordination of appraisal with other school developments is vital. A number of other national initiatives are already scheduled to impact on schools at the same time as appraisal. Some schools, particularly in the primary sector, will still be introducing local management schemes. The National Curriculum will continue to be incorporated into the school curriculum in different subjects and for different year groups. National Curriculum assessment is extending into Key Stages 2 and 4, and to the later foundation subjects.

Staff development for all these changes, together with any additional school priorities, should have been scheduled into the school development plan. Training for appraisal and its introduction has now to be carefully interwoven with these existing plans. Appraisal will be introduced over a four year period, and the school development plan should be looking ahead over that period to see how appraisal can best be phased in. Schools will need to consider how they can use the flexibility given within the Regulations. It should be employed, not to postpone the 'evil day' for as long as possible, but to avoid overload on staff in general and senior management in particular, and to make the best use possible of the training time and resources which will be available over the introductory phase.

In developing their strategies, schools will need to consider who should be trained, of what the training should consist, and who should undertake it. We now look at each of these.

■ Who should be trained?

There are training needs for all those involved in the appraisal process: appraisers, teachers and governors.

For governors, the main training needs are concerned with the provision of information. It is important that governors are clear about the scope of the appraisal of teachers, and the role that they will have in it. Such information will usually be provided by the headteacher, perhaps at a meeting of the full governing body. In addition to explaining the various elements of the appraisal process, it may also be useful to encourage an open discussion about the principles involved. At the end of whatever discussion takes place, it is essential that governors are clear that the appraisal of teachers will be carried out by the professional staff of the school, and that the governing body, or individual governors, will play no part in the appraisal itself.

◼ What training should be provided?

For teachers, training needs can be seen as requiring two phases: raising awareness and skills training. The skills required by an appraiser will be different, at least in degree, from those needed by a teacher being appraised. Nevertheless, we believe strongly that all the staff should be trained together, in both phases of training. There are two reasons for this view. First, it is important that the skills being employed by the appraiser, for example in classroom observation or in appraisal discussions, are understood by teachers as well as appraisers. Second, and more importantly, separate training of appraisers may create an 'us and them' feeling about appraisal, which is unlikely to reinforce the open ethos which we think to be so essential for a successful appraisal scheme.

◼ Raising awareness

This phase of training can be seen as having two aims:

- to ensure that every teacher understands the main components of the appraisal cycle, and what will be expected of them;

- to allow issues of concern to be raised and explored.

It is relatively easy to provide for the first of these aims. There needs to be an explanation of the government's requirements, with opportunities for clarification and discussion. There also needs to be an indication of the broad line which the school will follow in implementing these requirements. For example, who will be the appraisers, who will coordinate the appraisal process, whether there will be an appraisal working group to devise procedures, how staff will be consulted, the approach to self-appraisal, and so on.

Providing for the second aim may seem more problematic. There is a danger, of course, that allowing issues of concern to be raised and discussed may produce an opportunity for the moaners and cynics to dominate the discussion and, thereby, to generate a negative feeling about appraisal among staff. While this danger certainly exists, it should be possible to ensure that all are given equal opportunities to contribute to the discussions, so that a more balanced ethos is produced. The greater danger in our view is to proceed with the implementation of appraisal without facing these issues of concern head on, as this may allow distrust and anxiety to flourish. Remember that openness is the key!

■ Issues of concern to teachers

It may be useful here to consider some of the concerns that are raised frequently. These cover the following areas:

1 The purpose of appraisal

2 Confidentiality

3 Workload

4 Classroom observation

5 Meeting expectations

1 **The purpose of appraisal.** There is undoubtedly considerable concern about the real purpose of appraisal, fuelled by ministerial pronouncements about weeding out inadequate teachers. It is important for the headteacher and senior staff to reassure teachers that the main purpose as far as the school is concerned is to enhance professional development and, through that, raise the quality of learning experiences for pupils. Teachers should be reminded that there are clear procedures already for dealing with staff experiencing professional difficulties, and they should be reassured that there will be no direct link between appraisal and disciplinary procedures.

2 **Confidentiality.** Many teachers are concerned about the question of confidentiality. Who precisely will see the results of their appraisal? They are often apprehensive, particularly, about the role of the governing body in this area. First, the headteacher should remind colleagues that the governing body already deal with confidential issues relating to staff. Second, it should be emphasised that the chairman of governors will see only the targets derived from the appraisal process, and not the whole appraisal statement. The purpose of this is to inform school planning and not to identify failing teachers. There is, nevertheless, an issue here, and it would no doubt be reassuring if the headteacher were able to inform the staff that the chairman of governors had agreed to waive the right to see individual targets.

Reassurance may also need to be given about the security of appraisal documents. The use of a locked filing cabinet with the headteacher having the only key may serve the purpose.

3 **Workload.** The issue of workload is particularly sensitive at a time of rapid change and of increased responsibilities through, for example, the implementation of the National Curriculum. It needs to be explained that effective line management, in general, and appraisal, in particular, provides a mechanism for dealing with teachers' overload. Even so, there will be an increased workload because of appraisal, particularly for appraisers, and it should be made clear that the time required will be taken into account in the school's planning of its budget.

4 **Classroom observation.** Teachers are often worried about the classroom observation component of the appraisal cycle. There are a number of issues here, which need to be clarified. For example, will teachers be notified in advance? Who chooses the lessons to be observed? What criteria will be used to make judgements? What if the lessons are atypical? How often will observations be made? And so on. The central messages here are that observation will provide information for discussion rather than stark judgements, that visits will be made after negotiation between appraiser and teacher, and that observations will be based on agreed criteria on which staff will be consulted.

5 **Meeting expectations.** Some concern is often expressed about how the school will meet the expectations raised in appraisal discussions, particularly in terms of training needs and resources. It is essential to be honest here. Appraisers need to be clear about the parameters within which they will work, so that no promises are made which cannot be fulfilled. These parameters should be set squarely within the school's needs and resources, and expressed in the school development plan. Pilot appraisal schemes found that there was no increase in the overall demand for in-service training. Rather, the training needs identified were focused better on school and individual priorities.

▇ Appraisal skills

The skills needed for successful appraisal have been identified in Chapter 4. They include the skills associated with observing classroom practice and those needed in appraisal discussions. Like all skills, they need practice, and any training event designed to develop these skills will need to build in opportunities for practising them.

Of course, the best way of practising skills, and appraisal is no exception, is to do so in a real situation. Nevertheless, carefully planned simulations during a skills training programme can be of real value, particularly if there are opportunities to observe others using the skills, followed by discussion about what was observed. For each of the skills involved, it would seem sensible to have a brief introduction about what is required and then to provide opportunities to practise and, where appropriate, observe them.

In introducing discussions about self-appraisal, it is useful to explore some of the common problems which may be experienced, and which may reduce its effectiveness. There are two difficulties which can arise:

- teachers are unable or unwilling to see areas of weakness;

- teachers find it hard to say what they have done well.

The crucial answer to both is the need for honesty in self-appraisal. In the first case, improvement of performance cannot be pursued until the weakness is understood by both appraiser and teacher, and especially by the latter. In the second case, unwillingness to admit to successes will make it difficult to achieve an appropriate balance between praising and rewarding things done well, and working to enhance areas in which development or improvement would be beneficial.

Because self-appraisal is essentially a reflective and private activity, it is not appropriate to observe it in action. Instead, practice should be carried out individually. Each member of the group might be asked to spend fifteen minutes reflecting on the main areas in their jobs, how well they think they achieve in these areas, who knows what they do, and what other things they would like to do. The provision of a standard form to record responses will be useful here. Discussions about the practicalities of self-appraisal can then follow, based on perceptions of this exercise.

Training for **classroom observation skills** might involve an introduction of the major issues, perhaps involving a member of the local authority, and discussion about what form the criteria for classroom observation might take. It will not, of course, be possible to carry out observation of classroom practice during the formal training, but opportunities for joint observation of classes can be provided at a later stage.

Discussion skills are dealt with best through a brief introduction followed by practice. This practice can either be 'real' – discussing actual job performance – or 'simulated' – discussing imaginary issues. The advantage of the former is that it provides a more realistic context; the latter gets over worries about confidentiality. If the former approach is used, it is essential to stress that the discussions are absolutely confidential to the people involved in the discussion. One helpful format is for people to work in groups of three, with one taking the part of appraiser, one the appraisee, and one a non-participant observer. After the discussion, there should be an opportunity for the observer to provide feedback to the other two on how well they used discussion skills. The roles can then be rotated, so that each gets experience of the three roles.

Target-setting skills can be introduced by outlining the main criteria for effective targets – see Chapter 13. These can then be practised by providing information about a fictional teacher, and discussing in groups of three or four what targets might be appropriate for this teacher. The whole group can then meet to compare their ideas and discuss them.

■ Training for equal opportunities

In Chapter 4, we noted that men and women often bring different attitudes and stances to the role of teacher, and that this factor could well influence their approaches to appraisal. We recommend, therefore, that training for appraisal should cover the issues of equal opportunities and sexual stereotyping.

■ Who should undertake the training?

The Government has made some money available to LEAs for appraisal training through the GEST funding mechanism. Many LEAs will be using such funding to help establish a comprehensive training programme for their schools. This might consist, for instance, of briefings for heads and appraisal coordinators, training days for all teachers within a school, and background information and materials. Where such support is provided, it will undoubtedly at least ease the burden which the introduction and implementation of appraisal will impose on schools.

There will, however, be some schools which do not receive this degree of support. They may need to mount their own training programmes. In such cases, the following points should be taken into account.

The training programme should be prepared and managed in a thoroughly professional way. This means that the trainers must be credible. To achieve this credibility, they will need a number of attributes:

- the normal skills associated with INSET providers – experience in managing adult learning; an understanding of the nature of change, and strategies for bringing this about; and access to a range of training techniques and approaches;

- a comprehensive understanding of the subject of appraisal together with an insight into good practice;

- a knowledge of the school, its aims and objectives, and the position(s) from which the teachers start.

The above comprises a daunting list of qualities and skills, particularly when the number of tutors likely to be required is taken into account. If the trainers are drawn from outside the school, it is unlikely that they will have either sufficient time to devote to the needs of the school, or the detailed knowledge required about the school. If the trainers are drawn from within the school, they may have neither the necessary INSET skills, nor a detailed knowledge of appraisal.

We have already emphasized how crucial the training programme is to the smooth introduction of appraisal, and the success of the training programme will be highly dependent upon the proficiency of the trainers. The provision of high calibre trainers is therefore a matter which merits serious consideration from the senior management team. Ideally a cadre of trainers from within the school's staff should be trained. This would then increase the expertise immediately available to the school, as well as making the arrangement of the training programme within the school logistically easier. It may be therefore that schools who are without LEA support should seek outside assistance in obtaining initial training for their school-based trainers. These trainers could then plan and implement a school-based training programme. There are now a number of commercially published appraisal training packs which could assist them in this task.

15 Links with discipline, dismissal and pay

The government's regulations are very clear about the relationship between appraisal and discipline, dismissal and pay:

▶ **'Appraisal procedures shall not form part of any disciplinary or dismissal procedures ...**

'But,

▶ **relevant information from appraisal records may be taken into account ... in advising those responsible for taking decisions on the promotion, dismissal or discipline of school teachers or on the use of any discretion in relation to pay.'**

Open discussion between appraiser and teacher about the latter's performance requires the willingness of the teacher to face up to areas for improvement raised by the appraiser and the identification of weaknesses which the appraiser may not have noticed. If the teacher believes that this may lead to the withholding of annual increments, to a mediocre reference or to disciplinary procedures, then he or she is likely to conceal or deny such weaknesses. If this happens, then the essential trust between teacher and appraiser will be damaged, and the principal aim of improving performance will be endangered. We believe strongly that this is sufficient reason to make it clear that links between appraisal and pay, promotion or discipline should be discouraged.

Merely stressing to staff that there will be no direct links is unlikely to be sufficient. Each governing body will need to develop disciplinary and grievance policies, and a policy for remuneration of staff. These policies are likely to be successful if

- the staff are involved in their development;
- there are regular opportunities to review them;
- all staff are provided with copies;
- they make clear the use to which information from appraisal will be put in making decisions.

◼ Disciplinary procedures

The government Circular makes clear that appraisal should be *clearly separate* from disciplinary procedures, but that those entitled to access to appraisal information may draw on it during disciplinary procedures. In producing their disciplinary procedures, governing bodies should make this clear, and state how information from appraisals will contribute to the process. The local authority will usually produce model procedures, which will have been discussed with the relevant trade unions. It would seem sensible for governing bodies to consider these and either adopt them or amend them. If the model procedures do not contain a statement on the part appraisal might play in providing information for disciplinary procedures, one should be included.

Effective working relationships between a teacher and his or her line manager should involve the identification of areas of weakness. Such weaknesses should be discussed as soon as they become apparent; they should certainly not be kept until the appraisal discussion. The appraisal discussion will, however, provide a formal opportunity to discuss inadequate performance, to consider how performance might be improved, and to agree targets for action by the teacher specifically related to the areas of weakness. As with other targets, there is then a shared commitment to ensure that the targets are achieved.

Governing bodies and headteachers, like all good employers, should wish to encourage and secure improvement in teachers' performance, including that in areas of weakness. They should see the use of disciplinary procedures or dismissal as a last resort and, indeed, as a failure of the system to achieve the required improvement. It is important, therefore, to stress to staff that appraisal will not be used as a stick to beat them with, but rather that it should help to avoid the need for disciplinary procedures to be employed.

◼ Pay and promotion

The government Circular on teacher appraisal states there should be *no direct or automatic link* between appraisal and promotion or additions to salary. However, the suspicion among teachers (fuelled by various pronouncements by government ministers) that there will be linkage is likely to continue. This is particularly the case in schools where decisions about promotion and discretionary pay awards are already seen to be arbitrary or unfair.

What, then should a school do to convince staff that there will be no direct link? There are two ways of doing this:

- explaining how information which influences decisions about pay and promotion is obtained, and the part that appraisal will play in this;

- devising a policy for pay, which makes clear the criteria to be used.

The major source of information should be the day-to-day performance of the teacher. Without an appraisal system this may often be at best scant, at worst, plain wrong. Appraisal, because it encourages the appraiser to be more aware of the teacher's performance, can therefore be seen to provide more reliable and valid information. Also, because it focuses on improving performance and providing professional development, over time appraisal can lead to better prospects for promotion and for enhancement of pay.

■ An example of a policy for pay

In drawing up their policies on pay, schools may wish to consider the following example.

Introductory statement

The governing body recognises the central role of the staff – both teaching and non-teaching – in maintaining and improving the quality of education provided at the school for all its pupils.

In consequence, the governing body will seek to recruit and retain staff of the highest quality and to ensure that each member of staff receives recognition and appropriate remuneration for his or her contribution to the education of the pupils and to other aspects of the life of the school.

Aims

In developing its policy for pay, the governing body will aim to:

- demonstrate that it is a fair and responsible employer;

- provide equal opportunities for all staff, with particular regard to gender, race, disablement and age;

- support the long-term aims of the school, as expressed in the school development plan;

- produce a staffing structure which reflects the needs of the school;
- maintain appropriate pay relativities between posts within the staffing structure.

Discretionary awards

Use may be made of the following:

- incremental progression on the standard scale;
- temporary incremental enhancement;
- incentive allowances;
- adjustments to the salaries of the headteacher and deputy headteachers.

At present, the governing body does not believe that the resources available will permit extension to the standard scale; this situation will be reviewed in two years' time.

Temporary awards will be used for additional responsibilities taken on for a limited period. Such responsibilities will be linked to agreed priorities in the school development plan.

Because of the social and economic background of many of the pupils, and the high proportion of pupils from ethnic minorities, the governing body recognises the difficulty of recruiting staff to the school. It therefore proposes to offer maximum credit for previous experience and to give up to two additional increments to staff newly appointed to the school.

Withholding of annual increments will be considered only in exceptional situations.

Procedures

The governing body will ensure that:

- discretionary supplements to teachers' pay will only be awarded in accordance with agreed criteria;
- the criteria will be drawn up in consultation with staff;
- the criteria will be reviewed each year;
- supplements will be awarded in a fair, equitable and consistent manner;

- salaries will be reviewed annually; supplements will be awarded at the time of the annual review, save in exceptional circumstances;

- all information on vacant posts, allowances and enhancements will be made available to staff.

Criteria

The award of discretionary supplements to pay will be constrained by the overall amount of money available within the budget. Nevertheless, discussions about appropriate levels of pay will be based on agreed criteria, rather on the amount of money available.
The criteria will fall into two broad categories:

- those related to recruiting and retaining staff;

- those related to rewarding staff for their performance and responsibilities.

Some of the criteria will relate to the post held. These include:

- the level of responsibility, including the number of people managed;

- the difficulty of recruiting to the post.

Other criteria will relate to the qualities and skills of the member of staff, including ability as a classroom teacher.
The governing body will ensure that, in making discretionary pay awards, there is an appropriate balance between those for the level of responsibility of the post held and those for the qualities and skills of teachers.

Information used in making decisions

In advising the governing body, the headteacher will take into account information from appraisals, as well as other relevant information gathered, for instance, from the day-to-day management of the school. The governing body is convinced that appraisal should be aimed primarily towards the professional development of staff; as a result, there will be no direct link between the results of appraisal and pay or promotion. Equally, while appraisal will improve the information available for the writing of references for job applications, it will supplement existing sources of information, rather than replace them.

16 Monitoring, review and evaluation

The process of appraisal will take up a significant proportion of the school's resources, and these ought therefore to be used as productively as possible. This implies that there should be

- monitoring during the appraisal cycle to check that the various stages are being carried out to schedule and in line with agreed procedures;

- a review process to ensure that the appraisal procedures are as effective as possible;

- an evaluation process to enable the outcomes from appraisal to feed back into, and influence the development of, school policy.

Monitoring the appraisal cycle

One member of the senior management team will probably be responsible for coordinating the appraisal process in the school. He or she will need to monitor that process to ensure that it is running smoothly. This will include:

- scheduling all teachers for appraisal within the specified time scale;

- allocating appraisers to all teachers;

- ensuring that the appraisal process is being carried through – that evidence is being collected and that appraisal discussions are being held;

- checking that appraisal statements have been prepared, agreed and filed;

- forwarding targets relating to professional development needs, where this is appropriate, to the person in school responsible for planning training;

- checking that a review meeting is held during the second year of the cycle.

▣ Reviewing the appraisal procedures

In Chapter 7 we suggested that staff should be fully involved in developing the appraisal procedures and documentation used by the school. Similarly, we believe that the whole staff should be asked to help in reviewing the ways in which those procedures operate in practice. It is unlikely that any process will be perfect the first time through. Staff will be more likely to tolerate defects if they know that they will be given opportunities to comment and propose improvements. Even though such a review may be time-consuming, it will be well worth the senior management's time to collect staff feedback in a systematic way.

The collection of data might be undertaken in different ways. Questionnaires could be issued, one for appraisers, one for the teachers being appraised. A review body might be established which could interview a cross section of staff. Staff meetings could be arranged, on a whole staff or departmental basis, to hold structured discussions.

Whatever method is used, the various appraisal procedures should be reviewed in a systematic way. Below is an outline of the areas and points which might be included in such a survey.

- **Training** Did it prepare appraisers and teachers adequately for the tasks involved?

- **Preparation** Did the initial meeting enable an agreed agenda for appraisal to be established?

- **Self-appraisal** Were the forms provided helpful? Did the process contribute positively to appraisal?

- **Classroom observation** Was the process valid and were the observations representative?

- **Collection of other evidence** What other evidence was used, and was it fair?

- **The appraisal discussion** Was it positive and helpful in celebrating success and supporting areas of difficulty?

- **Target setting** Were the targets set appropriate and acceptable? Was training and support offered to assist in meeting them?

- **School or departmental policies** How might these need to change in the light of what has been learnt?

When data has been collected, it should be collated and analysed. This evidence should be used to judge which parts of the appraisal procedures have been successful and which now need adjustment. In some cases, further training may be required – observation or discussion skills, for instance, might not be fully developed. Some documentation may need amendment – the self-appraisal schedule, for example, might need refining. Or some of the processes may need clarifying – arrangements for the appraisal discussion, for instance, might require alteration.

The review process should therefore lead to a full audit of all appraisal procedures and documentation, resulting, it is to be hoped, in significant improvements in the second cycle.

■ Evaluating the outcomes of appraisal

The review procedure outlined above will not only give information about the appraisal cycle. It will also reflect on the whole spectrum of school policies and structures. If used appropriately, appraisal can form a beneficial part of the school's self-evaluation system and can feed valuable evidence into the policy formation process. We can look at how this might work in practice.

The job description is the basis of staff appraisal. The job description should define the teacher's responsibilities and duties, and appraisal should sample these duties on an agreed basis. The job description should grow naturally from the school's overall policies – it converts the school's objectives into duties and responsibilities for the individual teacher.

However, the appraisal process gives an opportunity to review that conversion. Does the job description still reflect the overall purposes of the school? Are there ways in which it could be modified better to serve the school's objectives or to use more effectively the teacher's talents and skills? The opportunity is also there to look at the appropriateness of the school's aims and objectives themselves. Are they still appropriate, or are modifications required to fit them better to the perceived needs of the children?

The main task of appraisal is to review the performance of teachers in the light of their specified duties. However, teachers can also review the appropriateness of those duties in the light of the school's objectives. At the same time, they can reflect on the suitability of the school's objectives in the light of their own perception of children's needs. Appraisal gives a chance not only to evaluate teachers' work, but also to evaluate the context within which they are working.

Appraisal will also include an evaluation from the teacher's point of view of the support received from the school, and its relevance to the teacher's duties. Thus the whole staff development policy is being evaluated from the classroom teacher's stance, and the degree to which it is helping staff to achieve the school's overall objectives.

A good staff development policy aims to increase the effectiveness of teachers. The policy should recognize that teachers work both individually within their own classrooms and as members of an overall team carrying out the school's curriculum and development policies. Appraisal can play a vital part in the development of an effective policy. Information about development needs will be generated for each individual teacher. The data can then be combined across the staff to give a total picture of the future development support which the staff as a whole require. Thus appraisal has the potential to create the feedback loop which will turn a top-down managerial model into one which is responsive to, and is owned by, the staff themselves.

A managerial model of staff development could well appear as below.

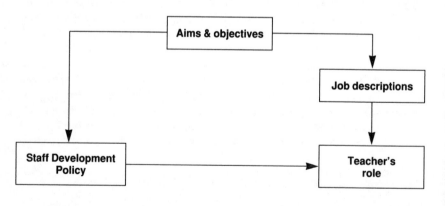

The introduction of appraisal, however, can introduce a feedback mechanism as shown on the next page.

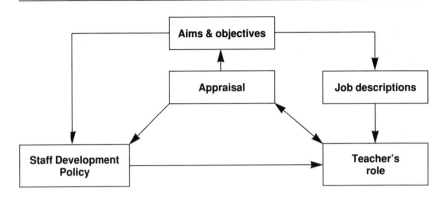

The appraisal process can tell the management about the effectiveness of the current staff development policy and can give firm pointers to the directions in which it needs to be developed in the future.

Of course, if this virtuous circle is to be established, there must be a structure in place through which the results emerging from the appraisal process can be considered. This is a delicate matter, for the appraisal process itself should remain confidential. Both the appraisal report itself and the annex containing the negotiated targets will be available to a strictly limited number of people. This confidentiality is essential to the atmosphere of trust in which appraisal should take place. It would be sad if this confidentiality acted against a proper use for evaluation purposes of the information arising from appraisal.

The Regulations already allow for the targets for professional development and training to be forwarded to those responsible for planning and training and development at school level. When schools establish their own appraisal schemes within the Regulations, they will need to consider how other information pertinent to the staff development policy can be communicated to those who need to know without breaching confidentiality.

The school will ideally need mechanisms which

- coordinate and consolidate appraisal outcomes in terms of: comments on the school's aims and objectives; the negotiated targets; identified professional development and training needs;

- review and amend the school's aims and objectives and the school development plan in the light of comments received;

- revise the staff development policy to take account of these changes and the identified teacher developmental needs.

17 Conclusion

In concluding this book, we think it is worthwhile reflecting on what research into appraisal has produced. According to research findings, successful appraisal is based on the following:

- an approach which is developmental rather than judgemental;
- clear expectations of what appraisal is intended to achieve, for both the institution and the individual;
- the maintenance of people's morale and self-esteem;
- a focus on behaviour rather than on personality;
- an open system, which is understood by all concerned;
- a clear policy on how appraisal information will be used;
- well-developed skills in appraisers.

We believe that all of these factors will prove to be as important in the appraisal of teachers as they have in other spheres.

We hope that this book has provided some insight into how these factors might be included within the schemes provided by local authorities and the detailed procedures produced by schools.

Index